INSTINCTS

Other Books by the Author

BLOOD FLOWER

ETMA PNIKRE

FORBIDDEN and UNHOLY SPECULATIONS

THE ASKANDAR
(A Journey Towards Immortality)

LOCK LINKED
INTELLIGENCE—INSTINCT—DREAMS—EDUCATION

INTELLIGENCE and INSTINCTS
(UNDERSTANDING YOURSELF AND OTHERS)

Editor of—KALEIDOSCOPE ONE

These Published Books are
available from the publisher as eBooks

◆　　　◆　　　◆

INSTINCTS

✦

The Hidden Spirits That Drive You

Norris Ray Peery

iUniverse, Inc.

New York Lincoln Shanghai

INSTINCTS
The Hidden Spirits That Drive You

iUniverse, Inc.

For information address:
iUniverse, Inc.
2021 Pine Lake Road, Suite 100
Lincoln, NE 68512
www.iuniverse.com

Front Cover Graphic is by the Author.
This print edition is Version: V-2.3

ISBN: 0-595-28278-4 (pbk)
ISBN: 0-595-74844-9 (cloth)

Printed in the United States of America

For

those very special persons who have

Inquisitive

And

Hungry

Minds

*Note: Whenever it is convenient,
this book should be read aloud.*

Contents

FOREWORD

Some of the material presented herein, has been published in a less detailed presentation in some of my earlier books.

So that we, more or less painlessly, come to a realistic understanding of the overwhelmingly powerful domination, which our inherited instincts have upon each of our lives, we will begin this tale of our instinct's hidden spirits in the manner of a wise swimmer, who not knowing the body of water in which they are about to plunge, come somewhat hesitantly up to the water's edge and cautiously every so slightly dip just the tip of their toe into the water as a means of testing the water's temperature. When the water's temperature is found to be within a survivable range, then the cautious person might slowly begin to enter the water and proceed into its ever-deeper places, but if it is not known what hidden secrets may lie beneath the liquid's surface, then caution is the swimmer's best companion.

Here, in the best sense, we will begin by dipping our mental toe into the first shallow waters of nature's world of instincts, because if we dive too quickly into the depths, we will have no wise appreciation of the majestic transformation from the shallows of other creatures to the depths of our own being. And so now you brave and inquisitive swimmers come to the water's edge.

INSTINCTS

ooooooooooooooooooooooooooooooooo

(Instinct: an inherited and essentially unalterable tendency of
an organism to give a specific response to an environmental
stimuli without first requiring analytic thought.)

THE ANT

For many of the simplest creatures of nature it is quite easy to observe and understand that most, and usually all of their life's functions are controlled by their inherited instincts. It is maybe easiest to believe that this might be true, when we observe some insect going about its daily activities. It is nearly beyond belief to see a tiny creature like an Ant, whose central nervous system's cells are countable in the hundreds, performing various exceedingly complex tasks.

Ants instinctively scout about their nest's nearby environment in search of food. When an individual ant discovers a food source, the Ant's body instinctively begins to actively secrete a chemical substance and then while the Ant is bring some part of the discovered food back to their nest, the Ant is at the same time laying down on the ground a chemical trail of substances secreted from its body, a chemical trail which leads like a roadway from the food's source all of the way back to the Ant's home nest. Immediately when other food-scavenging ants that are at the nest detect the fresh chemical roadway, which has been laid down by one of their fellows who has returned from the newly discovered source of food, those other Ants whose duty it is to scavenge for food are instinctively compelled, just as if they were non-biological mechanical robots, to follow the invisible chemical roadway to the newly discovered food. When they arrive at the source of food, each ant will bring what small amount of food that they can carry back along the same invisible chemical roadway, and at the same time they each lay down a fresh chemical trail for other Ants to use as a guiding beacon to and from the source of food.

Ants are instinctively drawn, by even the most unbelievably weak food odors that might be drifting in the air, to fallow those odors to their source. As an example: Wet food remains which are placed in a waste container in the cabinet under a kitchen sink, when the cabinet's doors are closed, the food odors build up their concentration within the cabinet's closed space and some of the concentrated odors might migrate through the small openings where the sink's water pipes and drain penetrate through the home's interior wall. The odors then slowly begin to fill the interior of the wall's empty spaces. Eventually, if there is even the smallest crack of an opening between the sections of the wall, then the

3

food odors migrate through these cracks and the odor's migration might eventually fill the complete length of the inner wall. If by chance there is the slightest opening from the wall to the outside world, then the accumulated food odor drifts through the opening to begin defusing into the air outside. Outside of the home's wall, any Ant passing nearby the wall, who is in its instinctive food-scavenging mode, upon detecting the slightest hint of the defusing food odor, will instinctively, automatically, and without choice follow the defused food odor towards its ever increasing concentration to where the odor is coming out of the wall. And if the Ant can fit through the slightest crack or opening in the wall, the Ant, in a like instinctive manner of a moth who is irresistibly drawn to a light in the darkness, will be irresistibly be drawn to enter the wall and follow the ever increasing concentration of the odor to its source at the waste container located in the cabinet under the kitchen sink. Once the Ant has discovered the food, it takes its tiny share and starts off towards its nest with the prize, as the Ant journeys back towards its home nest, the Ant lays down a nice fresh trail of chemical scent that the Ant's fellows at the nest can follow back to claim their share of the discovered food wealth. Of course the final outcome of this instinctive deterministic scenario is that a marching convoy of Ants follows the chemical roadbed back to raid the food source, but once the food source has been finally exhausted, the still continuing convoy of Ants who are following the invisible roadway to its end, find there is no food to be had at the trails end, then the Ants automatically revert to their instinctive random food hunting mode, and the multitude of Ants disperse from the location of the original food source in the cabinet under the Kitchen's sink. The Ants instinctively begin searching randomly throughout the house to discover any other food sources, which might be available. With the Ant's instinctive very sensitive ability to detect and to follow a food odor to its source, it is not too much time before the infestation of Ants has discovered every source of food in the house which has any aroma whatsoever, and also those other non-aromatic food sources such as sugar, which the Ants inadvertently stumble across in their random searching of the house.

Ants of course perform many other even more complex instinctively controlled functions, which are all directed without conscious thought, but whose direction and functioning is determined by a logic represented by fixed reflexive neural structures all of which are inherited, and whose functioning is switched on or off by simple conditions present in the Ant's environment.

Ants instinctively provide for the orderly enlargement and maintenance of their nest, the storage and hording of food supplies, the intricate care for their queen Ant who is the provider of Ant eggs, which are meticulously nurtured and cared for until they become adult functional members of the Ant's powerfully instinctive interlocked society.

You should realize that an Ant's instinctive physical and neural nature is meticulously interwoven, functionally, with the nature of its physical environment and disturbances within the Ant's environment can seriously disrupt its ability to function there. If an Ant's natural environment is in anyway disrupted beyond the realms where the Ant can instinctively function, then the entire Ant colony will move in mass to relocate at a more suitable location where their instinctive nature can fit functionally into that environment. If as an example an Ant's nest is grossly and over abundantly supplied with a food such as sugar, the Ants will leave their nest and relocate to an area where food is in a more natural balance with their instinctive nature for it being discovered by means of randomly searching for it.

The Ant has had no schooling. No fellow creature taught the Ant how to fulfill its mission of being a functional Ant. The Ant's life-long dance across the environment and its complex interactions within and with that environment are determined by the fate of its birth, solely by its inherited instincts. In the best sense, Ants are one of Mother Nature's evolutionary produced biological machines, whose every function is instinctively mechanistic, and they are creatures that are completely definable in mechanistic terms.

THE FROG

Frogs are amphibians and they are creatures that we might think of as somewhat more complex than are Ants. Here of course we are looking at a creature's complexity in terms of the comparative quantity of its basic neural structures coupled with the how diversified are the reactions those neural structures are able to exhibit, as compared to those same characteristics found within another different kind of creature. It is certainly the quantity of diversified reactions that a creature can exhibit that is the primary determiner of their comparative complexity. So by means of this rather simple minded method of a system for ranking the "Complexity" of creatures, we have a crude but functional way of comparing one creature of nature to another quite different creature.

The Frog, you might guess from its physical size as compared to the size of an Ant, might exhibit a proportionally much greater complexity over that exhibited by an Ant, but the physical size of a creature's body does not have any direct relationship to how complex a creature is compared to a physically smaller creature. If we itemized the reactions that an Ant or a Frog are capable of exhibiting, we might discover that these two creatures are of nearly the same complexity, but that their instinct's evolution has simply equipped them to survive in quite different kinds of environments, which relates directly to their differences of size. Both the Ant and the Frog are essentially creatures whose every action is determined by their inherited instinctive capabilities, which solely determine their every action and reaction for surviving within their environment.

When we looked briefly at the world of the Ant, it should have been clear that the Ant's instinctive functioning in its environment demonstrated a dynamic life style. The Frog's life is quite the opposite. The Frog's instinctive style, for reasons we will soon discover, is almost sedentary. This is easily understandable from the revelations made within a famous paper published in the late 1950's entitled "What the Frog's Eye Tells the Frog's Brain." It is evident from the findings revealed in that paper that a Frog's world consists visually of the most rudimentary remnants of the structures we humans can see existing in the real world. The Frog's visual world seems to consist of only the edges of those things that exist as complete objects. The Frog is essentially blind to the interior substance of an object and only knows, or sees, the object as its outline. So in the Frog's brain the real world as it exists for the Frog is predominantly outlines devoid of any interrelationship between the objects, which contributed their individual edges to form the Frog's visual version of the world.

The Frog's eye also has another ability, other than detecting edges, it has the ability to send powerful attention getting signals to the Frog's brain if any small object in the size range of an edible insect or worm, is moving either smoothly or erratically within the Frog's field of vision. Such objects are minimally representative of those small living creatures on which the Frog depends for a source of food. If an object within the Frog's field of vision is within certain size boundaries, independent of the detailed real world characteristics of the object, and the object moves, then the Frog recognizes it as potentially an object of food. The Frog has no other criteria for judging a small object other than its movements and its physical size. On the other hand, if a Frog is completely surrounded with its natural food and the food makes no movements whatsoever, then the Frog will never discover the food is present and could die of starvation while it was surrounded with edible food.

Like the small objects whose movement sends powerful attention arousing signals to the Frog's brain, the Frog's eye also generates powerful signals and sends them to the Frog's brain should any of the detected edges in its visual field begin to move with respect to the rest of the visual field.

And lastly the Frog's eye generates strong signals that are sent to the visual areas of the brain, should the intensity of a part of the Frog's visual field suddenly change by becoming dimmer than what it was previously. Becoming quickly alerted to any sudden change in the intensity of light such as a shadow appearing within some part of the Frog's visual field could be a strong indication that a predator was approaching.

Now lets consider a Frog as it sits peacefully on a pond's lily pad. The Frog sees the world around it as a composite of lines that have no representation of what edge boundaries they define. They are just a bunch of various lines. If the Frog has a nearly empty stomach and some object, which is within the correct size range which the Frog, by means of its instincts defines by its size and movement as food, the Frog will without any other considerations attempt to capture and consume the object. The Frog does not see any difference whatsoever if the object is a fishhook on a fishing line, a small lead shot on a line, a synthetic fly on a line or if it is a living free flying fly. The Frog has no ability to visually distinguish between any of these objects. The Frog's instincts driven by its rudimentary visual inputs swing into immediate action and cause the Frog to attempt to capture the object for food.

And if our Frog sitting on the lily pad has some shadow enter into its visual field, the Frog solely by means of its instinctive reactions jumps towards the darkest part of its visual field, which is nonmoving, as an attempt to escape from what might just possibly be a predator.

Even a Frog's sex life is completely instinctively determined. The female Frog is drawn towards her mate, solely by the sound of his voice. They are able to fulfill their reproductive function, once the male is located, by means of coming together in a direct physical contact where the male Frog climbs upon the female's back and rides her by tightly locking himself to her in a vice like grip by using his front legs. The male Frog does not perform penetrating intercourse, but remains on the Female's back until the time she begins laying her eggs at which time the male instinctively squirts his sperm onto the female's egg mass.

The Frog is totally driven in all of its actions by its inherited instinctive reactions to the sensed happenings in its environment.

THE
TRANSPARENT TIGER

We need to create some images within your imagination, and from just words you need to build those images with enough commonality that we are both essentially imagining the same structures.

Imagine a tiger as it slinks and then creeps through the grass as it stealthily sneaks up on its prey. Now imagine that you can actually see inside of the tiger, as if its body is constructed of totally transparent materials. Imagine you can clearly see, every bone, every muscle, the connective tissues, all of the nerves, and all of the tiger's internal organs. So as the tiger sneaks through the grass, you can see not only its exterior form, but also all of the synchronous functioning of its internal structures that are driving its life and its movements. You can see the tiger's heart rhythmically beating, and the tiger's blood as it surges in spurts through the tiger's arteries and eventually comes as a smooth continuous flowing river of blood back to the tiger's heart. You can see the tiger's lungs as they inflate and deflate with each quick shallow breath. You can see the different muscle groupings of the legs as they slowly and harmoniously contract or relax to cause the leg's bones to assume the ever-changing positions, which move the creeping tiger forward. You can see the muscles, which control the tiger's beautiful eyes as they compensate for the tiger's body movements to keep the eyes deadly fixed on its prey. Got the idea?

All right. One of the important things to understand from these images is that all of these physical aspects of the tiger, as it creeps towards its prey, are working together as a precise and harmonious unfolding of various related motions, which all taken together, are driven by the preprogrammed steps of an inherited dance, a dance whose harmonic musical driving forces, all come from the tiger's basic instincts. During the tiger's lifetime, it has through learning, refined the control of the those basic instincts it inherited at birth, and after a time the tiger has honed them into the most exacting controlled movements that have progressed the tiger from being a little playful kitten, to being a highly precision stealthy stalking and killing machine. By "machine," I of course mean a completely bio-logical machine.

Now let's form some new images. Images of what normally are not easily seen as parts of this same story. First realize, that all of the physical movements we have visualized, each and everyone of them, are solely driven by controlling sig-nals which come from nerves that are embedded throughout the tiger's body. And now imagine, that we can see the intensity of the commands coming along those individual nerves. We can see them as represented by an intensity of light originating in each particular nerve, light that represents both the command and its intensity, in terms of the light's brightness. Now with these ideas in mind, imagine again our transparent tiger. And without my saying in exact detail, imag-ine the physical motions and along with these images, imagine the light of vary-ing intensity coming along the nerves, as they are propagating the commands to the tiger's individual muscles, that are driving all of the tiger's discrete individual motions. Hopefully, You should be able to visualize this, not in a way of exact-ness, but as a general self made image of the relationships of muscle and organ movements all directed by the controlling nerves, which so finely, so precisely, so harmoniously orchestrate this whole scenario of the tiger's every movement. You should be able to visualize in your imagination a continuing complex symphony of light that flashes, flows, fluxes, and ebbs throughout the tiger's body, and this visual, ever shifting, ever harmonious resonance of the tiger's various different instinctive mechanisms as they radiate their commands through the tiger's ner-vous system to control every part of its body, this image is one of the most com-plex and magnificence displays of Mother Nature's designs of any that could be witnessed any place in the universe. The only problem is we can't actually see it happening, we have to generate the imaginary images of what is happening within in our mind.

We've looked into the transparent tiger and we've seen in a general way by using our imagination all of the various physical and neural functions that are taking place as the tiger is stalking its prey. If you could watch the transparent tiger for a complete cycle of its daily activities in the same way as we have in this first imaginary instance, you'd discover that all of what you beheld was causally driven by the tiger's basic instincts, whose controlling instinctive nerve impulses have all been modified, tuned, and refined by memories which the transparent tiger had learned during its lifetime of living within its natural environment. I mean by this, that what the tiger is, is completely definable by its instincts and the things it has learned, but you need to remember that it's all inseparably inte-grated within the tiger's physical body. If this seems too finite, too limiting and if it's difficult for you to believe that all of the actions of a beautiful creature like a tiger can be reduced to its memories and instincts, then realize that I'm not completely reducing the tiger to memories and instincts. I'm just saying that its life motivating and driving forces can be reduced to that. Of course the tiger is the complete creature, but it is its memories and instincts, which define it as an individual tiger, separate from all other tigers. So what you need to comprehend is, if this is the true situation, for the tiger, then it is important to realize that this generalizes to creatures other than our transparent tiger. I believe you can realize what some of the implications might be, and without the slightest doubt, they encompass all living creatures of nature, of every kind, including us.

All right, what we have so far considered is that the tiger is a physical biological package, the tiger's overall body. And the physical package contains other aspects that cannot be equated to the majority of the substance, which makes up the tiger. These other aspects consist of three things. I have so far mentioned only two of them. They are the tiger's inherited instincts, which direct every life function of the physical body that houses them. Yes, I mean every life function, but I need to hedge on that just a bit. So leave me a little room to wiggle in. The second definable, but ethereal thing to consider in the tiger's make up, is all of the things the tiger has learned during its long life within its environment. And those things, which have been learned, modify, and modulate how the basic instincts exert their control over the physical body. So realistically speaking in many cases, what has been learned can aid in driving the tiger. But it is always the instincts that sit between the physical body and the learning. So we have a kind of **instinct sandwich**, where the bottom slice of bread is the physical body, and the upper slice of bread consists of the memories of everything the tiger has learned, and in-between the slices are all of the tiger's inherited instinctive mechanisms.

Consider now for a moment the instinctive nature of a domesticated cat, a companion, sitting on your lap and the cat is purring, singing its song of contentment and its acceptance of you as a friend, but seriously realize that if you were very small, say the size of a mouse, then no matter what you might do or how fervently you pleaded, that cat would attempt to catch you, maul you, and finally it would eat you, or at least eat most of you, because that is the instinctive nature of cats. The cat is dominated by its evolutionarily established carnivorous predatory instincts. They are Instincts, which are triggered into being activated by simple conditions such as smell, size, and movements, much in the same as we saw that some of these same kinds of stimulating elements triggered the Frog into exhibiting its instinctive eating reactions. When these three elements are all in agreement in the cat's mind, they indicate to the cat that it is food that has been detected, and this simple combination of sensory detections will trigger the cat's basic instincts, and no matter that you might, in your tiny form, be singing an opera, or dancing a ballet, or any other non-mouse like performance, the cat will instinctively catch you and eat you.

THE HUMAN

We should now truthfully begin to recognize that within some of the simplest creatures of nature, their reactions to situations in their environment can be seen as solely driven by their complex repertoire of inherited instincts. Hopefully, we can also begin to realize as we examine the slightly more complex creatures that their actions are also instinctively deterministic. Then as we look further to ever increasingly complex creatures, if we are truthful with ourselves, we must come to a realization, that there are no sharp boundaries between creatures, which can set any creature outside of the evidence, which with certainty points to the instinctive domination of the actions of all of nature's creatures.

At the beginning of this book, part of the definition of an instinct is: **"An instinct is Essentially Unalterable,"** but by this statement it is meant that **the "hereditary nature" of an instinct is not subject to being change by any socially exerted controls or by any kind of learning. However, during an individual's lifetime many aspects of the expression of some parts of their instinctive nature can be successfully modified, by being enhanced, or by being partially or completely subdued, and this ability to modify an instinct's expression is of a primary importance for all individuals who desire to live within a more or less civilized and somewhat peaceful society.** Some instincts have been so enhanced by dedicated learning that they are evermore miraculous than nature's original intended purpose. Dedicated learning as a means of modifying and fine-tuning an individual's instincts produces the glorious diversity in which our kind sometimes finds great delight in exhibiting and witnessing.

OUR INSTINCTIVE NATURE

Like all inherited traits, different individuals who carry a trait manifest it in varying degrees. The intensity of an instinct's observable display, always exhibits itself at some intensity that lies within the broad range of possible intensities that can be seen represented within the overall population that inherited the instinctive trait. Even inherited physical characteristics, such as blue eyes, are represented by a broad ranging intensity of blue, from being barely detectable as blue, to ice blue, gray-blue, or dark blue. Even the inheritable diseases are represented within a broad range of how each particular individual manifests the characteristics of the disease. In some cases the disease may take a swift course and completely ravage the individual, while in other persons the same disease may proceed very slowly along its course and never reach a catastrophic intensity, and there are those persons who physically or mentally may never show the slightest detectable sign of their having the inherited condition.

So for every instinct, we must remain constantly aware that the magnitude of the instinct's observable expression within any individual lies somewhere within the spectrum consisting of the overall possible different magnitudes of its expression.

We should within this light of our understanding of the range of the expression of an instinct's traits, also realize that the borderline between what are considered to be normal mental characteristics and abnormal behavior should be seen as a much more flexible situation than has usually been the case. Some characteristics, which some persons consider to be "Abnormal", are characteristics that are necessarily found to some degree in most other persons within the population who are considered to be normal. The characteristics, which we overly generalize by labeling them as "Neurotic" or "Insane," are found to some minor degree in most persons within the population. It is only those persons who intensely display these characteristics that we mark with the generalized term "Insane."

Somewhat separate from the mechanisms of the brain, which make up its functions of intelligence are the inherited neural and chemical mechanisms that only exhibit themselves as instinctive actions or reactions. Many of the complex instinctive reactions, which we are able to witness and to attach a label that somewhat identifies them, are made up from a series of discrete instinctive mechanisms which are each successively triggered one after another from some initial triggering sensory event. When a complex powerful primitive instinct is triggered, the various mechanisms that compose the instinct spring into action one after another until the total elements of the instinct have been activated to produce the final observable result.

Besides remembering that the magnitude of the expression of an instinct lies within certain boundaries, it is very important to always keep in mind that the magnitude of a sensory event, which is able to initially trigger an instinct into becoming active, also lies within a spectrum which contains all of the magnitudes for triggering the instinct as are found within the individuals of the general population. From this we should understand that some individuals within the population are extremely sensitive to having certain instinctive reactions triggered from the weakest of sensory causes, and some other individuals within the population are nearly immune to ever having a sensory stimulation, which is powerful enough to trigger the same instinct. So the possible triggering level for a particular instinct is to be found within a spectrum of triggering intensities and that spectrum is naturally found within the boundaries of some bell curve, which represents the different individual triggering levels of the entire general population.

We need to consider the complex characteristics of instincts in the light of what we can see within the physical characteristics of a creature's nature, including ourselves. Consider the wondrous complex material features of our physical nature, the Eye, the Hand, the Ear, the Foot, the Mouth, and all the other marvelous complex organs that make up our bodies. Each of them was worked for millions of years against the fabric of the environment, where they were molded by "Master Mother Nature" to give us, each creature, a magnificent physical harmony within the complex material environments of nature. It is easy to look at the human hand and marvel at its wondrous subtle physical complexities. Just by means of visual observation, we can with ease see the hand's external structures. By means of medical dissection we can reveal the hidden physical mechanisms, which allow the hand to mechanically perform its functions.

All of the physical features that make up our bodies are relatively easy to see, but **the features that make up the complex mechanisms, which identify our instincts, are invisible to the eye; they lie almost totally hidden within us.**

The mechanisms of instincts are nearly ethereal things, whose presence is embedded within the subtle connections between nerves, muscles, and glands, all submerged within the intricate protein chemistries that bathe them.

Instincts are real things, but their invisibility allows them to escape counting. Instincts are powerful things in their own way. They are as powerful as any physical extremity. They are as much a physical and permanent part of every creature as is any Hoof, Trunk, Eye, or Arm. Instincts are as powerful in guiding the activities of a creature as the muscles and structures of a leg are at predetermining how a creature will walk and run.

We must always be careful when analyzing the actions of any creature and ignorantly attributing those actions to free choice, when in fact they may be totally deterministic and solely driven by instincts, as can most clearly be witnessed in the actions of the Ant and the Frog.

I would propose that nature's evolution has endowed each and every creature with a repertoire of instincts, which if countable would approximate in number the distinct countable physical features of each creature. It should not be too difficult to believe, that during the millions of years of the evolution of the various physical features of nature's creatures, that the evolution of each creature's instincts was not also taking place at a comparable pace. And with a bit of reasonable suspicion, we should be willing to consider that the human creature is also heavily cloaked, even saturated, with multitudes of major and minor inherited instincts.

Instincts move our kind, and each of us as individuals, down pathways that were determined for us by a past hidden in the "Ancient Prehistory of Evolution."

Although the Ant cannot look at it's own actions and see them as instinctive, as deterministic, you would think that we as creatures of a higher reasoning power might be capable of examining our own actions and seeing the truth of what is there. **But it is more to the truth that we see within us the forest of our actions, but cannot see the trees that make that forest. In many cases it is true that we see what we want to see, nothing more, because we refuse to look in detail, and we are fearful of what truths might be revealed.**

We often hear that we as humans have not been present in the environment for more than maybe a few million years. This might be true, but we and those creatures who are our relatives, our direct line of relatives, have been evolving in the environment since the very beginning of life on this Earth. Our direct line of relatives forms a continuous sacred chain of life that leads from life's earliest beginnings to connect unbroken directly with each of us.

I believe that we should try to understand, that **most all of our "Instinctive Nature" was determined long before we became Homo sapiens.** It is certainly most likely that we share with the other creatures, in varying degrees, many if not most of our instincts, and the variance of intensities of expression of those shared instincts ranges from nearly no expression to a hundred percent expression. Certainly within the other members of our family of apes we can see most of our instincts are also represented among their kind. Certainly within the other mammals, we can see that we have many instincts in common with them, and so, even within the most distantly separated families on life's evolutionary tree, we share some of our, and their, most basic instincts.

As an indicator of how we might proceed at identifying what are our different instincts, and just how numerous they are, we might think about this proposed axiom:

Every reactive attribute, which is common within and throughout our kind, and is not a learned attribute, is necessarily an instinctive attribute.

We will on some few occasions make use of this axiom when deciding for or against some attribute being or not being instinctive. We should also mention that any attribute, which has an extended commonality that can be seen to exist in other creatures that are different and separate from humans is a further guarantee that it is an instinctive attribute.

Try to understand that our "Instinctive Nature" is mostly composed from instinctive mechanisms that gave our most distant ancestral predecessors some advantage for survival within an environment that was savagely hostile, and that today**, we are creatures wearing a "New Thin Skin of Civilization," which we have wrapped around us as a camouflage for the still primitive instinctual animal that lies beneath that skin, and as a camouflage of certain aspects of the nature of that animal, which we ourselves do not want to see or admit is actually there.**

You may wish to believe that the following instincts are not in anyway a part of you, but the truth is, that to one degree or another, they are in fact an inseparable part of your being, and their hidden spirits invisibly guide your life.

There is no way to understand the nature of a problem, our problem, and to seek a reasonable solution, if we are unwilling to admit to the existence of the problem.

Now we are ready to begin our mental swim into deeper waters and to begin considering some of our kind's discernable powerful instincts, which although hidden beneath our skin are tightly woven throughout every fiber of our being, and secretly guide each of our lives in ways we might never have guessed was possible.

THE HARD SURVIVAL
INSTINCTS

And so, let's peek here-and-there beneath our skin of camouflage and see what might be hidden there. We are creatures of a generally weak physical design. We have no great teeth for the biting and the tearing of flesh. We have no razor sharp claws with which to hold an opponent at a distance and no swift legs to carry us faster than the leopard and not even a powerful sense of smell to tell us the faintest hint of what is drifting in the wind. As compared to many other creatures, it would seem that physically we were at a great disadvantage for surviving in a vicious and wild primitive world. It would appear that in a primitive world of physical struggling, we didn't have a chance for surviving. **But here we are, "Supreme Survivors of it All," survivors who now sit atop the Heap of Time, and we wear The Thin and Gentle Skin of Civilization as the Badge of our Ultimate Success. How can this be? We are often taught, that we are near descended from angels, but in truth, we as creatures of Nature's Universe, unlike the Angels of Myth, are the most Dangerous, Most Potentially Vicious, and Most Deceitful Creatures in Existence. We have at our very core, a powerfully Savage Instinct.** Our own-recorded history bears truthful testimony to this fact of our nature. This truth is found in the endless piles of tortured and mutilated bodies that are stuffed into and dangle from the pages of the books that record our history. Savagery is there in our history from our earliest records and continues to the present day. Savagery is a primary and inseparable part of our "Instinctive Nature" and it accompanies us throughout all of time, ready to be called on at a moment's notice to release its power in the name of survival. Many scholars, philosophers, and others go to the greatest of extremes in their attempts to convince us that we are not savage at all, but instead we are gentle social creatures. But today's world has regurgitated multitudes of bodies that had been secretly hidden in the sands of prehistory and we can now see into our most distant ancient past, and there we can see the evidence of the unbelievable savage tortures and death that humans ritually executed upon their own kind. There is no speculation of savagery here; the evidence is there in the mummified, strangled, hacked, decapitated, and mutilated bodies yielded up from our most distant past. Keep in mind that our brains, our intelligence, and our instincts have not changed at all, since those times of primitive atrocities to our present day. We are now the same creature as those of our kind who practiced their ancient religious sacrificial atrocities against helpless individuals.

Many people like to believe that these savage powerful mean traits are only to be found in others, whom they can point their fingers at, while denying that they are present within themselves. There are those, who would like to believe that only others could commit atrocities, and that they themselves could never do such things. It is a direct consequence of such a personal denial that the savage instinct can survive hidden inside of us until some unusual circumstance causes it to be violently released from what was a seemingly docile person. There are those, who like to believe that a good civilized education can calm the beast inside, that an educated person is a reasonable person and can by use of reason free themselves from their "Savage Instincts." But the verifiable facts from recent history tell us that many of those persons, who have committed the most terribly vicious crimes against their fellow human beings, have been highly educated persons, who loved and patronized the fine arts, and were loved and respected by the members of their family and were also respected within the religious institutions of their society.

It may be true that in some persons, the nature of the vicious savage creature sleeps so deeply as to not be easily awakened, while in others it lies nearer to the surface of their nature and is ready to jump out of its hiding at the slightest provocation.

Primarily in males, but to a lesser extent in some females, we find the physical abuse of their partner in marriage or in other kinds of personal relationships is all too common within today's societies, but in truth we can reasonably assume that such abuse in not new to our time, but has been a common feature within most all past societies. Partner physical abuse is essentially absent within some very few societies, where a kind of complete sexual freedom is both allowed and encourage between all sexually mature members of the society. Those partners who have or are experiencing physical and/or mental abuse often testify to the intricate deception an abusive partner is willing to use to hide their Savage Instinct, which periodically gets completely out of control and where sometimes the abuser, after the abuse has been inflicted, makes sweet talk about their devotion and love of their partner and sincerely promises that the abuse will never happen again. The abused partner must come to the truthful realization that the abuse is solely the representation of their partner's Savage Instinct and that it is as much an integral part of their partner's character as is their partner's physical arms or legs, and without medical intervention their partner's savage instinctive abuse will never be subdued. It is unreasonable to hope or to believe that the Savage Instinct can be indefinitely subdued solely by means of psychiatric therapy, any more than it is reasonable to believe that such therapy can cause a patient's leg to slowly shrivel and eventually disappear. The elements, which make up the Savage Instinct, are so inexplicitly woven into every part of a person's being that they are not subject to any effectual modifications except by continual and lasting interventions.

It is those males, wherein the Savage Instinct lies near to the surface of their general nature, that are the ones who are the usual perpetrators of violent physical and mental abuse within their personal relationships and within society. Most probably the only safe and sure way of changing the nature of those persons, who have repeatedly demonstrate during their entire lifetime that their Savage Instinct is on a short fuse, is by the use of mood altering medications, which to control the instinct would need to be administered for most of their lifetime. The medicating of those persons, who demonstrate over-and-over-again that their savage Instinct is dangerous to society, is the best sure way that society can be safe from their terror. Medicating is a much more reasonable and cost effective solution to this problem than the other alternative, prison.

The Savage Instinct is most likely controlled by the body's chemistry coupled with triggering patterns from the environment and it bows little if any to intellect. The fact of the matter is that for most of us, who live in mostly reasonable and secure and sane environments, we never encounter those events or strings of events that would trigger our primitive Savage Instinct. **But for those who meet face-to-face again-and-again with unbearable fear, humiliation, inescapable threats, or are in any way physically or mentally terrorized, then if there is anyway possible, the beast that is the "Savage Instinct" will sometimes finally rise up in vengeance against their oppressor or cause them to flee away from their oppressor.**

During times of war, we can most easily see in many individuals, that the "Savage Instinctive Beast" has been fully unleashed. After each war's end, it is usually the custom of those who are the triumphal winners to ask how could any group of people have possibly participated in the atrocities that were committed during the war by those who were eventually defeated? It should be more to the point to ask, given the orchestrated arena of fear and hated that institutions propagated against certain groups, how could the people not have participated in ignoring or committing the atrocities?

We sometimes see the Savage Instinct raging in individuals living in an otherwise peaceful society. Once the Savage Instinct has been released within an individual, the vicious acts performed sometimes become self-reinforcing. It is always the case that when some individual exhibits vicious instinctive tendencies, everyone is asking the same questions. How can this be? What has caused them to do it? Was it their parent's fault? Was it because they didn't go to church? Did they have a bad childhood? Was it because they were a loner? And on-and-on the same questions are asked over-and-over. It is in the act of asking these questions, that the askers believe they are distancing themselves from any probability that they could have done such a thing; that they could have ever committed such atrocities. Their reasoning is that it was because of some kind of insanity or there was some most exceptional cause, which drove the person to commit the vicious acts. It is a way for the casual observer to continually deny the basic nature of the Savage Instinct, which is actually what is behind the vicious acts. It is how the individual says, without actually stating so, that nothing could possibly drive them to committing such savage acts and that they have no claim to a personal Savage Instinct.

It is the custom of societies to continuously work at subduing the Savage Instinct within the population. Societies attempt to accomplish this goal by making heavy penalties for those who commit acts of violence. This method is somewhat successful in the general case, and because it is generally successful, we might be led to falsely believe that the Savage Instinct is not a basic part of the entire population. But, now consider the interesting situation, where there are no strong penalties or taboos against a certain kind of antisocial savage violence that takes place vicariously in the playing of certain video games. The players of these games enthusiastically engage in vicariously committing what most educated and reasonable persons would consider to be the most repulsive acts of violence. The very large numbers of people who willingly play these savagely violent games, is an undeniable testimony to the fact that the Savage Instinct is alive and well within our general population. Many other and more realistic exhibitions of violence are allowed within some societies, violence such as, boxing matches, so called extreme physical combats, the public viewing of the torturing of animals such as dog fights, and cock fighting exhibitions, bull fights, and in some cases, the public execution of persons by hanging, firing squads, decapitation, or electrocution.

It is the general case that individuals in society are forbidden to physically exhibit their own savage instinct; so as a means of placating their natural savage desires, they instead vicariously worship at the temples of

violence, where violence is offered up to them in copious amounts through the mediums of books, television, video games, and in motion pictures.

Sadly for those who worship at the temples of violence, the good old times of the grandiose violent exhibitions at the Coliseum in Rome are long past. Probably at no other time or place in recorded history has there ever been a more conclusive example of the presence of the Savage Instinct within the human population, than was demonstrated by those who were a part of the Coliseum's show and those vast numbers of persons who were its willing witnesses.

Good economic times within a Society are a balm that tends to hide the Savage Instinct by never allowing it to be called to the surface of our personalities. Even captive tigers are contented and docile creatures when they are well feed and sheltered. But, when that economy that provides so well for them fails, and they become hungry, the Savage Instinct comes immediately to the surface of their personality. So also for humans in times that are economically difficult, or because of war, or other stresses, the Savage Instinct is on a short trigger for being released. In the best of economic times it is natural that crimes, of all kinds, including crimes of violence decrease. The simple truth is, this is equivalent to the times when the tiger is well feed and cared for. When the worst of economic times are at hand, all crimes including crimes of violence will necessarily increase and there are no numbers of police or other forces that can change that situation. Many times attempts at using excessive force to control the rise in violence might just help to aggravate the violent situation. Such times, when the Savage Instinct is freely and strongly raging within the population, are times that are ripe for violent social unrest and even social and political revolution.

The fact that some societies are willing to allow their governments to implement the death penalty is itself a testimony to the existence of the Savage Instinct. For society, the death penalty is their way of exercising their Savage Instinct while believing their hands are clean of any involvement, and that they are just simple gentle creatures. It is of course the officials of government, who are too weak, and fearful of the potential political consequences, to speak out against this people's morbid circus of pretended justice, and who are unwilling to stand up against this example of the most savage will of the people, which allows it all to continue.

As concerns the Savage Instinct and children, we should understand that children act, just as families and society allows them to act. If we allowed it, children would instinctively be happily torturing, mutilating, and murdering each other. A situation that was believably portrayed in the book, "Lord of the Flies." For the Savage Instinct to be somewhat subjugated in the adult world, it must first and foremost be subdued whenever and wherever it shows its viciousness within our children. Not subjugating some of our most primitive and antisocial instincts as we see them first raising their ugly head during childhood is surely going to become an evermore-potent curse upon our society's future. Children must be disciplined, for their instincts are totally blind to their own future consequences.

As long as we as a people, continue to deny that the Savage Instinct is really a part to one degree or another of each of us, we will never find success in understanding our nature or in finding some reasonable means of controlling of it. We will continue on into the future, wringing our hands in futility while trying to understand how such savageness can continue to stalk a civilized people.

There is an instinct that in the past served us as well as the fiercer instincts. Today that instinct, in many cases, works against our best hopes. I speak of the instinct that is our kind's natural attraction to be a part of a herd. Herds are of many types and sizes, at one extreme end of the spectrum there are the small herds that you might like to call a group; then at the other extreme end of the spectrum there are the largest herds that are called nations. Herds exist in every size and variety: the family, the tribe, the city, the religious group, the police, the professional associations, the teams of sport, and all of the special interests groups. You may prefer to use the expression "Social Group," because it has a gentler, a more civilized sound to it. But, I think it is more to the point to use the cruder sounding word "Herd" as it is more to the point of what in modern times is really going on within the social structures of the herd, and it gives a rightful feeling about the word and the imagery it brings to mind is directly relatable to the other animal herds of nature.

Every herd is made up of a group of individuals associated together with a body of knowledge, myth, or ritual. The group of individuals that make up any herd consider themselves to have become a part of the larger organism that is the herd. When an individual joins a particular herd, they assume the mantle of the myth that belongs to the herd. That mantle of myth (or knowledge) in most cases is something that the herd has acquired at great cost over long periods of time. It is always necessary, that to belong to any herd, the individual must meet the entry requirements of the herd. The "Herd Instinct" drives each individual towards belonging to the most powerful and prestigious herd to which they can gain entry. In belonging to the most powerful herd, each individual member acquires a feeling of maximum security and maximum individual worth. Individuals in their desire to become apart of a large or otherwise powerful herd are often times willing to sacrifice there position within any smaller herd of which they are a member, this is true even when it might mean sacrificing their membership in their family, as we can see is often the case in times of forceful social conflict. But, most individuals are driven by their natural instinct to become a member of some kind of herd, even if it is only the immediate family, or the minimal next step up from the family herd to some religious herd, or maybe to become a member of a neighborhood gang.

Belonging to a herd has served us well during the prehistoric and early historic times. Much of what our kind was able to accomplish could only be done by large groups of people laboring together at hunting, farming, soldiering, providing domestic services, or building. But now, machines accomplish much of what could previously only have been accomplished by a large group of persons laboring together.

Now in our present world our Herd Instinct, from which we cannot escape, is making much of life more and more unbearable. Throughout the world our cities are bursting to hold the great herds of people inside of them. For most crowded cities, their peoples are continually spilling out into the surrounding areas. Some herds are so large that many of their individual members can no longer identify with the herd in a manner that is satisfying to their instinctive needs. Instead of the individual feeling a part of the herd, many persons feel lost, smothered, and neglected by the herd. And most individuals, needing desperately to belong to some herd, join smaller herds in which they can more personally identify and satisfy their needs. Too often in our present world, too many of our kind, because of educational and/or economic reasons, are only equipped to join herds that are at the bottom of the social ranking, and so particularly in areas where the economy is weak or dead, neighborhood gangs proliferate. Of all of the modern problems related to the Herd Instinct, the problem of gangs is perhaps the easiest to solve. Yet, because of our ignorance about the most basic instinctual causes of the gang problem in our present society, we are prone to foolishly try to breakup the gangs or to forcibly subdue their members. We in our blindness try to destroy the only herd where these needing individuals are able to satisfy their unknown hidden desires to be a member of a protecting herd. Almost any alternative to the gang herds, which can give an individual a feeling of being strongly bonded with a group and also where the individual feels needed, is sufficient to solve this problem of gangs. We would, if we were actually a society of reasonable people, spend the necessary effort of time and money towards eliminating some of the forces of social and economic segregation and other injustices that are the causative roots of the gang problem. Solving this problem, by expending whatever effort it takes, is more to society's long term advantage than is the continual never ending waste of time and monies at forever battling to subdue a result of a basic instinct which is nearly impossible to ever be completely subdued, instead of trying to subjugate this unacceptable display of a natural instinct, the power for the instinct must be redirected by offering up a kind of herd which is more acceptable to a civilized society. Such a herd must be of a minimal complexity, where the individual members can find a place where their own contribution to the herd is seen by them to be noticeable and relevant. It probably is an appropriate time that a new herd that caters to the extra social learning needs of children and young adults is established, a herd that is more sophisticated than the present day Boy and Girl Scouts of America. In reality the present day organization of boy and girls scouts is in most all cases just an extension of the local religious organizations that provide meeting places and mentor the scouts, while at the same time, they work relentlessly at instilling within the scouts the religious organization's own particular local and religious biases. We need a more modern and open minded organization in which our youth can participate free from the two thousand year old biases that are out-of-step with our understandings of today's world. It needs to be a national organization, a herd, where the diversity of our society is accepted and honored, a herd that has a strong appeal for the young persons of both the urban and rural environments. It should be a herd where the individual members can seek and obtain real expertise in the specific areas of their interest, instead of the minimal knowledge gained in obtaining some kind of scout's merit badge.

Some of the reasons why persons become members of particular herds are easy to comprehend. People feel safe when they perceive rightly or wrongly that they are among a group, which is made up of individuals that represent what they have been taught to think of as their own kind. So from this we see the most common stable large herds within every multi racial or multi ethnic society are those herds where the members share, a common shade of skin color, or a common ethnic heritage, a common language, a common dialect, or share common mythical beliefs.

There is a primitive and strange attitude concerning self-defense and the defense of other members of a herd. Sometimes when a herd consisting of great numbers of animals is around an African water hole, and lions attack some of their members, the herd takes minimal action to escape the situation. It's as if they instinctively understand that with so many of their kind in the immediate area, the probability, that they themselves will be attacked and eaten by the lions, is very low. And we see the members of the herd will persistently stand docilely nearby while the lions consume one of their kind, and the members of the herd show little or no concern. But when the situation is different and the herd of animals at the water hole has relatively few members, and lions attack them, all of the members of the herd scurry to escape. In this case, it is as if the animals realize there is a high probability of their own personal danger of being captured and eaten by the lions. We should give some consideration about how these two different situations reflect on our own understanding of the public's apathy sometimes shown by crowds of people in our great cities who are willing witnesses, and yet they ignore the crimes of violence that are committed in their very midst and before their open eyes. Those same violent crimes would not usually be allowed to happen unopposed within the confines of a few witnesses within a small town, where the victim is a known member of the community, a member of the local herd.

Individuals, who feel insecure in their individuality, especially need the strength of some herd to give them a feeling of worth. Many kinds of herds are important structures within society in that they can be powerful bonding agents that contribute to social order and stability. But herds in this modern world also have a darker side. It is sad to note that it is a serious major fault of the herd and particularly of the individuals who are members of the herd, that they sometimes work at making individuals that are not members feel fear for their expressed individuality. Members of many herds work relentlessly at putting down any person who is not a member and with whom they come into contact on a daily or frequent basis. We often can see this relentless conflict against nonmembers of a herd carried to the extreme. Within other creatures of the animal kingdom, it is not uncommon that the nonmember of a herd is tormented and murdered. When we witness such an event between other members of the animal kingdom, we sometimes conveniently forget that our own kind sometimes demonstrate the same kind of relentless harassing, torment, and too often in the past it also involved murder. We only have to think back to the not so distant goings on in the Southern United States, where many individuals, who did not and could not belong to the then dominant herd, were systematically harassed, tormented, dehumanized, and too many times horribly murdered, and it was all executed with the knowing and enthusiastic approval of the gentle members of the dominate herd.

Between two different herds, we can sometimes witness a kind of protracted warfare, which rumbles on-and-on at a barely sustainable kind of minimal battling. This situation is commonly found wherever two primarily different religious herds are each distinctly gathered into their own location, but are also located within the immediate proximity of each other.

There is an almost magical and nearly universal power of persuasion that is inherent within even the smallest of herds. There are examples from experiments conducted within groups made up from seven or eight people. Within the small group, all of the persons, except one, know of the experiment's planned deception, which is to be perpetrated on the one unknowing member of their group. A questioner, who is not a member of the group, asks the members of the group a simple question to which it is quite certain that every member of the group knows the correct answer. But the question is directed to each member of the group individually and asked lastly to the unknowing member of the group. Each member of the group individually responds to the question with identically the same answer, an answer that is to everyone an obviously incorrect answer, and when the last member of the group is asked the same question, they in almost every instance replay with the same answer that the other members of the group gave, even though they understood that their answer was not correct. And after the experiment was completed that one person admits, they knew that the group's and their answer was incorrect, but they followed the group's answer, because they didn't want to appear as different from the others of the group, the herd. Here in this experiment we can see the power of "The Herd Mentality." **This same oblique power of the herd's persuasion is the force that directs armies into suicide advances, and pilots into being Kamikaze pilots, and many a victim into laying themselves across some sacrificial religious alter.**

Members of herds are fiercely protective of the mythology of their herd. They are protective of the herd's mythology to the point of being both totally unreasonable and cruel to anyone who would challenge it. You can see this to be true even within herds, which most persons might consider to be the nobler herds, the medical associations, philosophical, religious, scientific, and the arts. It is only necessary to look at what is happening within nations, between nations, within religions, between religions, within the institutions of medicine, science, and the schools to see the defining evidence of the herd's conflict with different herds and with the any individuals within the herd who show their personal desire to be different. In almost every field of human endeavor, we see the Herd Instinct leading almost all down some common trail with a joyful willingness to trample anyone who would dare to deviate from the path. Even if the leader of the herd has some fruitful insight to where they are leading, it is a disaster that all should follow without seriously questioning or searching for alternative paths.

In our society, we are forever preaching the value of the individual, but if anyone actually dares to be that, to be an individual different from the others of the herd, then the herd tries to enthusiastically trample that individual underfoot.

Such a herd mentality costs humankind a great and unreasonable price in every field of understanding and discovery. Millions upon millions of dollars are forever being funneled into certain areas of medical research, where thousands upon thousands of people are supposedly expending a great effort at solving a medical problem. But after many years of funding, many multitudes of persons working and taking home a nice paycheck there is not found a solution to the medical problem, this is surely a result of the herd mentality, where the entire research army has forever been marching down one or few paths for discovery. It is the very nature of greet herds to intellectually flow within the main stream of thought and because of this instinctive nature, our billions of research dollars are usually swallowed up by the blindsided members of the herd who willingly skirt by vast numbers of potentially rewarding insights that could most probably lead to the solution of the problem.

We cannot change the underlying cause of the Herd Instinct, but we must modify its damaging results on modern civilization. **The herd always rushes to trample anyone that dares to be different. It is not, in recent times, to the Herd Instinct that we owe any salute for our civilized successes. It is to those very few, who have risked and escaped being trampled, that we owe our salutes and gratitude.**

There are just a few notable exceptions to the "Everyone be and act just like everyone else in the herd." One exception we find in the herds we know as musical ensembles. These herds are the world's best examples of how individual differences can be the herd's primary substance of value. Within these herds, individuals are encouraged to play their different musical instruments to their best perfection. It is by the controlled summing of the differences of sound produced by the herd's individuals, which produces the glorious sound of their music.

The greatest influences on almost everyone's life are the mythologies, philosophies, and fads of the herds. Nothing else, including family and/or schools, has such a powerful almost unshakeable influence on the individual's actions and way of thinking. There are only a few ways to interrupt this unholy influence that dominates the thinking and actions of what the Universal Creator surely meant to be a free individual, as a person who should be able to powerfully discover their own direction and joyous path through life. **Since it is instinctive that the herd has such a great controlling influence on the individual, it is by making use of specially designed herds that we can give back to the individual their individuality.**

Most creatures have an Instinct to Survive. This instinct is apparent within the monumental struggles, which creatures willingly make in their attempts to escape from bodily harm, either by putting up a violent fight against their oppressor, or by fleeing from the battle scene. The Instinct to Survive gives us the willingness to struggle for our survival, even when the obvious odds against surviving are monumental.

The Instinct to Compete is common among many species, but it rises to a kind of a warped perfection within humans. The Instinct to Complete, as it is generally seen in the animal kingdom, is about sexual competition to win a mating partner, and in this case we can readily see, it is an instinct whose primary drive is associated with the Sexual Instinct. In humans the true nature of the Instinct to Compete is also probably and primarily about sexual competition, but its basic nature has been so warped and contorted that it encompasses competitions that are difficult to relate by any observable means, which can demonstrate cause and effect, back to its surely sexual nature. Competition is a primary element of the capitalist economic system, and surely hidden there beneath all of the ruffles and flourishes, the basic competitive drive is still surely sexual.

The senses of every creature are basic and exclusive mechanisms for detecting the patterns of the real world. Each of the senses surely must have associated with them a long list of instincts, which have slowly evolved along with the sense's physical and associated neural structures.

The sense of hearing and its associated mechanisms that allow sound patterns to be stored within a creature's memory have an exceptional instinct embedded within their structures. This instinct facilitates certain kinds of differential hearing. I would guess that parts of this instinct are at least as old as are the first creatures, which were able to utter sounds as grunts or groans.

The mental mechanisms involved in hearing are very much concerned with discerning the finest details of any nuances imbedded within sounds. The major parts of any communication by means of sound must fall upon the sense of hearing and its associated mechanisms like a ton of noisy rocks. It is within, what might seem as the most minor nuances of sounds, where complex creatures have hidden their subtler meanings. We might think of the major sounds of a spoken language, as attention getters for the subtler sounds that lay nestled among their rocks. The major sounds are oft times the crier that points the general direction to the sweeter sound meats, where much valuable species specific and nearly mystical information resides.

We need to take note, that there are strong differences between the methods of communicating a language, which is both spoken and written, and there are accompanying great differences in how a person understands and reacts to these two different ways of communicating.

Seeing a written word with the eyes and reading that word, causes the word's pattern information to reach a person's memory storage area within their brain, which is reserved for patterns that have been detected by the sense of sight. Hearing the same written word, as a spoken word, causes the patterns representing the spoken sound to reach a different memory storage area within their brain, which is associated with their sense of hearing.

I propose that creatures, which have even a minimal spoken language, including any means of communicating by sound, have associated with their Sense of Hearing a "Differential Hearing Instinct" that is exceptionally powerful at detecting what we might believe are the most minor nuances hidden within the major sounds of their audio communications.

The Differential Hearing Instinct is capable of detecting even the slightest dialect or accent, which displaces the sound patterns away from the strict core sound of the common language or communication. Each individual intelligible word of every spoken language has subtle sound characteristics attached to it, which are unique to the person who is speaking. These subtle sound variations, embedded within the primary sound of a spoken word, allows it to be identified within a strict objective core meaning of the word, allows it to be identified as some displacement from the core meaning, allows it to be identified as belonging to the individual who speaks the words, allows it to be identified as to the speaker being within the group of the family, or within a group of friends, allows it to be identified as being a member or nonmember of the tribe or group, or identifiable as being a member of a nearby tribe or group, or as being foreign to all of these. There are many other nuances embedded within the sounds that embody a spoken word. These other sound nuances associated with a particular word might stimulate sexual arousal, or slide the core meaning of a word towards it being understood as a threat or challenge, or shift the sense of the word's meaning toward it being comical, or can color the word to stimulate many other varied emotional conditions within the listener. By means of the subtlest changes in the tonal quality of a speaker's voice, they can communicate directly to the listener's instinctive emotional centers, and in this way the speaker can communicate more than any words by themselves can communicate. There are those persons, who are so masterful at this technique of coloring the meaning of a spoken word that by their reading of the names from a telephone book; they can bring laughter, joy, or tears of emotion to their listening audience.

We can understand from our own memories of sounds, that the voices of the members of our families and friends or any familiar persons, are stored in our mind, and most importantly that the nuances, which uniquely identifies each of them and causes them to be discrete individual voices are preserved within our memories in appropriate detail. When we recall from memory any words spoken by a familiar person, we recall that memory as if the person was actually speaking; we hear their particular voice within our mind. We do not hear only the words of the speaker, but the words as if they are being spoken with the actual voice of the speaker, as we have remembered that voice. This is a strong testimony that the Differential Hearing Instinct is very much concerned with the sweeter meats hidden amongst the burden of the sound's rocks. We should be sure that this Differential Hearing Instinct allows for all creatures, the pinpointing and capture of powerful sound messages, which contain information that lies outside of the sound's primary or core meaning. And so it is believable, that when the lady frog listens to the chorus of male frogs as they are singing their mating songs into the cool night's air, she hears within one individual's voice the subtle sounds different from all the others, and that one different male Frog's voice commands her to find that one, the one who has rang all of her hormonal bells and filled her with delightful yearnings to be close to him.

So, it is also true that for our kind, the simple sound of a voice from an unseen person can trigger strong reactions about the desirability or undesirability of that unseen person.

We cannot here consider all of the instinctive biases that might be associated with language when it is communicated by sound. What we do want to consider is how this Differential Hearing Instinct might give some insight into an important social problem of our time and in fact throughout all of time. We need to consider some aspects of how and why this instinct is so important to our own kind. It is surely as important in similar ways to other creatures.

The main differences of real instinctive importance that separates individuals within or between races are not the color of their skin, their facial features, their hair color, the shape of their eyes, or any other physical features that persons normally associate with marking an individual as undesirably different from them. These features, which many tout as marking the differences between so-called races, which are not races at all, or ethnic groups, and as being the main identifying features that allow individuals the grounds on which to discriminate against each other, are not what I believe underlies the most basic nature of social discrimination. The fact is, that within any group we find that these individual physical features exist as a continuous morphing across the group. Also, as a whole, these features in varying degrees are pretty well common to us all. There is no single physical feature or features among them, which makes them grossly abhorrent. There is no physical feature among them that should inherently cause anxiety, hatred, fear, or social rejection. **The simple fact is, that social prejudices that are every-day associated with an individual's physical features are not in anyway derived from a natural origin. They are solely perpetuated as a socially learned bias.** These kinds of physical prejudices are uniquely the result of herd biases. The herds continue to foster these biases within society, because they see that in doing so, there is some special advantage to their herd. In the forthcoming section dealing with sex and sexual preference, you will realize that these prejudices concerning physical features have exactly the same origin and reasons for their continuing and unnatural survival within a society, as do those prejudices concerning sexual preference.

The Absolute Single Greatest Difference that Exists Between Humans is Language!

If we consider the nature of the spoken language there are some interesting considerations that might help us understand both the nature and reason for the biases that lead to discrimination against certain groups within a society. Consider that as primitive creatures one of our prime fears must have been a fear of being destroyed by our own kind. To attack and destroy a nearby group was a relatively easy means of acquiring both their material goods and more importantly to acquire their territory. Many other creatures in the animal kingdom strongly guard against these unwelcome and feared intrusions into their territories by members of their own species. For humans this was most certainly true during those most primitive times, when different factions were becoming more and more successful, therefore allowing the size of their groups to grow. It is the case between groups living in relatively close proximity that they are groups that have the most similarities in a common spoken language. But it is the nature of a spoken language, that children learn it from adults. It is this kind of learning that gives each group their own special dialect or identifying accent. This dialect remains a mark on their language as long as they stay generally separated from other groups that speak the same language. Some groups that foraged and wandered over areas that were adjacent to the territories of a nearby group encountered each other for only the briefest periods during a year, simply because of restraints upon food supplies which could not generally support the gathering together of a larger population. Remaining separated for most of the year, probably allowed the groups to maintain distinct spoken language nuances. It must have been from the most primitive times that the distant sound of a different dialect was an early warning of a possible impending attack. When hearing your own spoken language even from a great distance, you are able to identify the speaker as being or not being a member of your group. It is not difficult to believe that an important factor contributing to our survival was to be able to distinguish between the dialectical nuances of the spoken language. Since this differential hearing instinct is commonly found in other species scattered throughout the animal kingdom, the beginning roots of its distant developmental origins within our kind must be very, very ancient. It must have been the case over a long and extended period of our primitive history, a period long enough to establish that we have an instinctive uneasiness whenever we detect a dialect that seems to be close enough to our own primary language and different enough to alert us to the dangers of a possible attack from a neighboring tribe or group. It was probably true that during times when food supplies were sufficient, nearby groups had infrequent but good relationships with each other. On the other hand, when food supplies were in very short supply for long periods of time, it was the nearby groups that must have been the main competition, a competition that was about life and death, about the survival of the families and friends within the group. The result is, even now, when we hear such dialects of our common language, the instinctive bias raises an automatic prejudice as a sense of anxiety, an uneasiness that seems to reside as some irrational feeling deep down in our gut.

We might wonder why we don't have strong instinctual biases, prejudices, against groups that speak languages that are totally foreign. It is simply because for most all of time, we never had any contact whatsoever with such groups. They were so separated from us by great distances, that there was never any contact with them. There was no means by which to develop an instinctual bias. They were not a threat. We had no fears associated directly with any such sound patterns that lay completely outside of our known language patterns. We also have no instinctive bias against the songs of birds, the crowing of the cock, the call of frogs, or the communications of other creatures that have not regularly posed a dangerous threat to us. We do have biases against those creatures, which make sounds of communication that we can identify with threats to us as individuals, or to our group. If you are alone in the wilderness, the sound of the hiss of a snake, or the roar of a lion, I assure you will raise within you an instinctive fear that rattles uncontrolled within your guts. It is easy to see in other animals, how they instinctively respond to sounds, which for ages of time have denoted the presence of a nearby threat.

Consider an interesting thought experiment and see what conclusions we might draw about these propositions. Imagine the situation where by coincidence two individuals, one a Caucasian and the outer an African American, and who speak a common language and both of them have the same dialect as society's most dominant group. Assume that they were previously unacquainted with each other, and then for some undisclosed reason, they come into verbal contact by telephone. Imagine they are separated by such distances as to not allow them to meet or see each other. We put on them these two conditions, that they do not ask questions about to which ethnic group they belong, and that there is nothing within their conversation which would disclose their ethnic group. And I tell you, as an observer of this situation, that these two persons each have strong personal prejudices against the ethnic group to which the other belongs. In such a situation, where each of them can only learn about the other by what is said, by voice tonal qualities, by linguistic style, and all of the nuances that are possible to convey by the human voice, then these two individuals will begin to discover each other's interests and personalities. The subtle communicable voice qualities are all controlled by the learned patterns that are stored in their individual memories. As the contact between these two persons continues, both of the individuals are simply revealing to each other information about their life. They also might have instinctive reactions to the substance of their communications. If their communication persists for enough time, the individuals, as we say, get to know each other, and to understand to what degree they believe they are each similar or different. Such a contact, which can only involve the exchange of general information, with no knowledge of the physical characteristics of the individuals is enough and a sufficient way of establishing a relationship between these individuals. The relationship that develops between them can range across the entire spectrum of mutual acceptance or non-acceptance. But it can only be based on what they have communicated by voice. It is not too difficult to believe, that as long as the information contained in the tonal qualities and substance of their communications does not alert either of these two, that they each belong to an ethnic group, which they are prejudiced against, then, they could become friends, especially if the general information that the two exchange indicates that they are enthusiastic about the same interests in life and are emotionally and intellectually compatible. They might even become strongly bonded as friends. What should be said about this situation, if after these two by means of their communications become strongly bonded friends, and then they are allowed to meet face to face?

I cannot say that the Differential Hearing Instinct is the only element that contributes to and prolongs the unreasonable prejudice that exists between some groups in a society. But I do believe that it is the primary one, the one that clearly connects our automatic instinctive fears from the primitive past to the modern world. Of course, there are all of the unreasonable and unjustified hatreds that herd institutions and some individuals relentlessly work at attaching to the Differential Hearing Instinct, and it is interesting that they do become attached, but all of these can easily be shown to be without merit. They are things that are testable and rationally verifiable. But the curse of the instinct is that its strength generally cannot be controllable by means of logic, and so as long as the conditions persist that trigger the instinctive reaction, the biases, the prejudices, that have been associated with it will survive.

Babies and very young children sometimes are very fearful and cry when they are in a safe environment and are introduced to a stranger. We usually believe that the child is upset because they visually recognize the person as a stranger, and are therefore afraid of the new face. It is more likely that the stranger has spoken, and the child immediately recognizes that the voice is coming from an outsider to their known group of family and friends.

It is most probable that the Differential Hearing Instinct had its basic origin, far, far back in our kind's past, back to times when those distant relatives, who were eventually to become our kind, used it to gain a great advantage in their daily struggles to survive.

The sound of a spoken foreign language we may hear as curiously unusual or funny, but when persons, whose native language is the same as our own language, speak our language with an unusual dialect, we hear it as a dialect that represents the speaker as different from us, one who is not a part of our group, our herd, an "outsider," who appears to be masquerading as one of our kind, and who, according to our Differential Hearing Instinct, is clearly not one of us.

The Differential Hearing Instinct is very strong within the communities of other vocalizing creatures, who span across a great range of evolutionary complexity. It is an instinct, which is very strong in the other apes, marine mammals, and even birds. These other creatures will many times gang-up and attack any individuals who, by means of simply communicating by sound, have alerted them, that they are an intruder. Humans have at times demonstrated their willingness to flock together and rain terror onto individuals who are outsiders in a like manner of the other wild creatures.

We can many times see in the modern world that individuals, who belong to groups that have strong social prejudices against them, are able to integrate into the general society and be both successful and accepted if their spoken language and its nuances correspond to those of the dominant group. I would further suggest that, no matter what may be the outwardly visible physical characteristics of an individual, if we observe that their vocal speech patterns seem to be identical to ours, and we detect no accent or dialect, we automatically feel at ease with them, and feel that they are one of us.

We can also note that if a speaker has the physical characteristics of one ethnic group, but speaks with the accent of a different ethnic group, we have a tendency to identify them with the group associated with their accent and not necessarily with the group whose physical features they represent. Many times in observing such a situation we find ourselves momentarily with an uneasy confusion until we inevitably feel comfortable when we are resolved to associating them with the group represented by their dialect.

It is curious that biases are so attachable to this Differential Hearing Instinct. They can be biases that contain either negative or positive feelings towards an individual or a group. It appears generally that the biases that give a positive feeling are associated with those accents that originate from a foreign language, and that biases associated with local accents are almost always felt as negative, this is likely so, because local herds have taken it upon themselves to attach poisoned thoughts to the accents of persons who are not members of their herd.

You might be more willing to accept how the Differential Hearing Instinct is tied directly to the hidden strings that emotionally affect us, by considering how deeply the sounds of a musical score can touch and arouse our deepest emotions. Singing is a most powerful way of using the differential hearing instinct to communicate human emotions, which are completely independent of the comprehension of the words of the song and whose most powerful communication is made by means of the tonal qualities of the singer's voice. This is why a song performed in a language that is unknown to a listener can still convey powerful emotional feelings. Some musical artists of the voice or some other instrument can literally attach, by means of the nuances within the tonal quality of the music, some of their own inner feelings, which gives their music a personal signature, and these musical artists are the ones who are strongly accepted by their faithful audiences. It is not the music, but the musician's love of their instrument and the music, that is so powerful a means of communicating emotions of a depth that cannot, in any other way, be conveyed by the mere written notes or words of a song.

There are those who propagandize that a nation should not try to educate their children to speak a common national language and dialect, but should also teach by using some different language, which is a common language in some minority population within the nation, and to encourage tolerance for different dialects. But language, spoken and written, is our primary means of communicating with our fellow creatures. So if this encouragement for accepting dialectical differences within the spoken language has any real substantive merit for society, then it must also be true, that we should encourage and teach such variations within the written language. And every ethnic group should be encouraged to use spelling and grammar that is to their own desires and different from any national norm. I hope we can realize that such a wish-washy situation would become a disaster for any nation's language. **If it is true, as I believe it is, that strongly negative and unnatural biases and feelings can become associated with the sounds of uncommon dialects and accents within a common language, then to overcome these unreasonable instinctive biases, a nation must educate its population to speak a common language, a common spoken language that is recognizable by the ear as friendly, because even its subtle sounds are recognized as those of the national group.**

The Territorial Instinct exists and is strong in many of nature's creatures and is no less strong within our kind. It is an instinct that has served each creature well. The instinct is directed, in the most general case, to the protection of a territory where a creature gathers or stores food, where it might have a safe sanctuary for protection against the elements of the weather, and a place of protection for the raising of their young. It is a territory, wherein a creature's needs for sustaining its survival are to be found, a territory that creatures instinctively see as belonging to them, and where their Territorial Instinct leads them to attempt to exclude other creatures of their own kind, and any other creatures that might infringe upon their perceived rights of ownership.

For humans all of these reasons for exhibiting a Territorial Instinct are also valid, but for us, the Territorial Instinct is extended beyond the primitive natural land, where we found our sustenance, to include those territories that exist only within our minds. We are ready to defend our perceived physical and philosophical territories within our work environment. We are ready to defend those territories that contain all of the various properties that we directly own or dominate. We are ready to defend those territories of the mind that we embrace as theories. We are ready to especially defend those territories of the mind that encapsulate our mythical religious beliefs.

We even have our individually perceived territories within our homes, and these are those places where some family member feels they are the dominant or prime resident or owner of some definable space, although other members of the family may not be excluded from such areas. Serious temporary conflicts can arise between friends or a family member, who seems to be threatening an occupation of another person's home territory. It is usually the case in such conflicts, that they arise very suddenly, and their primary substance seems to have arisen from some disagreement that is in no way related to the Territorial Instinct, when in reality it is the fundamental cause of the hostilities.

Some of our greatest problems, involving physical conflict and social violence, come about when we are involved in defending the territories that only exist within the mind, and we falsely relate them to territories of the geography.

Many creatures have an instinctive paranoia. For those creatures, which we sometimes hunt as a source of food, when we see that they are exhibiting their natural paranoia, we sometimes falsely believe that they are wise creatures in the sense that they showing their intelligence for being ever suspicious of their surroundings. Paranoia is not a part of intelligence; it is a form of emotional nervousness. Paranoia, as it is represented within many creatures, is a very powerful instinct, which has always been a strong contributing factor to their long-term survival within a hostile world. Many different kinds of birds exhibit their obvious paranoia, Crows and Ravens are notorious for forever showing their caution, their paranoia, when they are not in flight, but are on the ground, where they are susceptible to unseen dangers.

The Instinct to be paranoid, like all other instincts, is expressed by different individuals within a population in various degrees of its possible intensities of expression. We, all of us humans, exhibit paranoia to some degree and for most persons their intensity for expressing paranoia lies within the central part of the bell curve, which represents the total range of intensities for expressing the instinct. For those persons whose intensity for expressing this instinct is represented at the lowest end of the curve, they are persons who seem to be unsuspicious of the consequences from any environment independent of however threatening it might appear to other persons. Then there are those persons, whose intensity for expressing this instinct is represented at the extreme upper end of the curve and their reality is about seeing the world in terms of what they believe are the real potential dangers that lie within all parts of reality and which other persons have been blessed to be oblivious for knowing. For those few persons within the population for which the intensity for expressing the paranoid instinct is at its maximum, they are in a condition of mind, where every object, condition, or event that is in their surroundings is seen as fear inducing. It's a state of mind, of unnatural realizations, which cannot be maintained without eventually resulting in the individual's final destruction or their complete mental withdrawal from the real world. But for most parsons in the population their paranoia lies somewhere safely between these two extremes.

There is an instinctive part of us that is interested in discovering the consequences of the destruction of real objects within the world. Even in small children, you many times see that when one child has patiently constructed some object of their desire, another child will joyfully destroy that object. It might seem inappropriate to some that there is a feeling of joy associated with the act of destroying. It is probably this feeling of joy that is the Destructive Instinct's driving force. In part, the personal joy or satisfaction, which comes when committing an act of destruction, comes from the individual's experiencing the dynamic consequences of their own personal power in action.

The Destructive Instinct, within a modern society, is an instinct that needs to be placed under the strongest restraints, if only because the machines and other instruments we have at our command with which to implement destruction are of such an awesome power in comparison to those which were available to our ancient ancestors. In warfare, we can see the Destructive Instinct freed to work its most terrible results.

The Destructive Instinct is an instinct whose consequences are not all completely negative. Many things will only reveal their inner structure and any treasures that might be hidden there, if they are broken open or destroyed. The mere destruction of objects must have led our ancient ancestors to the discovery of otherwise hidden sources of food. Also, the attempted destruction of small rocks must have been insightfully revealing, when it sometimes produced useful rock scraps with their sharp cutting edges. The smashing together of rocks during the nighttime or in the darkness of a cave must have reveled a sight of wonderment as the bright sparks from those impacts streaked through the darkness. The attempted destruction by burning might have been our first introduction to the cooking of foods. The attempt at destroying by the smashing of seeds, nuts, bones, and shellfish was surely our beginning at a primitive kind of food processing. Destruction by the methods of smashing or burning surely has contributed to many discoveries that have served us admirably. The attempted destruction by burning within a fire of shiny metals not only must have been the means by which we discovered that metals melt, and also upon their cooling they assumed the shape of the object in which they solidified. This was a most important discovery as it eventually led to our ability to cast tools from molten metals, and this discovery opened the door to stronger and more useful tools than those made from rock, which for centuries was the hardest material from which we were able fashion tools.

Many creatures other than humans use the destruction of objects as a means of getting at certain foods. We can see that some birds learn that to drop certain nuts or marine shells from a great height onto a hard surface is their best method of obtaining the food that is hidden inside of such strong enclosures. We can see that the sea otter learns to swim on its back while smashing a shell-covered sea-food against a rock the otter has placed on its chest.

Destruction is a process, which we humans still use today in attempting to discover of what things are made.

INSTINCTS OF THE NEST AND HOME

Probably one of the most important instincts, which has contributed to the survival of many different creatures, is the instinct of some parents to supply the most basic requirements of life for their young until the time their young are somewhat able survive on their own. This Instinct to Nurture is widely spread across many species, but is most highly developed in the most advanced creatures. In some mammals the instinct has evolved to such an extent as to become an extended nurturing, which greatly exceeds their young's most basic requirements for surviving. What nature's evolution has found to be a good thing has been exaggerated and extended in hopes that "more" must necessarily be better. Good old Mother Nature really doesn't work that way, but extended nurturing certainly is better than minimal nurturing, which only provides the most basic sustenance and a token protection from the elements of weather and from natural predators. Exaggerated nurturing extends itself from simply providing the minimal needs for survival to include guiding the young in their discovery of new patterns in nature, patterns usually only known by their adult populations. Sometimes extended nurturing, as it can be seen in the human population, really pushes the limits of the basic sustenance nurturing which nature intended. In humans, we see such occurrences as the nurturing bond between a parent and their child, where the parent refuses to be separated from the child even though the child has reached adulthood. We also see an unusual consequence of unnaturally extended nurturing in the case of the mother who encourages her child to nurse at her breast for ten years or more. The mother and child are unable to see anything wrong in this extended natural breast-feeding, and it is of course neither right nor wrong, but it is an extreme aberration of the extended Instinct to Nurture, and it will probably have unexpected future consequences for the child, because at a child's age of ten years, such breast-feeding seems to be an act that some persons might see as approaching an incestuous relationship. Certainly if a child was found to be breast-feeding from their mother after the time the child had become sexually mature, the act might well be thought of as being sexually improper.

Extended nurturing's most obvious success within human societies is seen in our social institutions, which are devoted to assisting our children at learning some of the vast amounts of knowledge, which has been accumulated by our kind during the past centuries from where our ancestors passed their discoveries forward in time by means of a spoken and written language.

The Instinct to Nurture is not only about nurturing our own offspring, but is a general instinct, which sometimes is extended to include other of nature's creatures. We can see this is true in how we care for those creatures that we have as our pets, a case were we have accepted another creature to live their life with us, and they have accepted us to be with them. It is sure that there exist many instincts, which are common between our pets and us. We should suspect that the commonality, of certain major instincts within them and us, is what has successfully brought us into each other's lives. The Instinct to Nurture causes us to see our pets as being a part of our overall family, and we sometimes think of, and act as if our pets are our children. The Instinct to Nurture is not a one-way affair extending only from us to our pets, but is clearly a two-way instinctive emotion, where our pets attempt to nurture us by the best means they have available to their kind. The strength of the Instinct to Nurture's establishes a powerful bond between our pets and us. A bond that grows ever stronger in accordance with our ability to be astute enough to truly understanding the nature of our pets, and our ability to respectfully allow them to be, and to honor the fact that they are unique creatures of nature, and though not human, they have their own personal dignity. We often times see just how strong these bonds can be, as is demonstrated over-and-over again by a pets willingness to risk their own life in an attempt to save the lives of their human friends. We also see that humans are many times willing to risk their life by coming to the rescue of their own pets and other creatures that are discovered to be in some kind of eminent danger.

There are stories from the past, which are intended to show the mythical powers of cross-species nurturing. Many of the most ancient religions have stories of their heroes, of one kind or another, who were in their infancy succored and raise by some real or mythical nonhuman creature. There is the well-known story of the ancient founders of the Italian city of Rome. In Roman mythology there is the story of Romulus the founder and his brother Remus who were rescued from the Tiber River by a she-wolf who suckled and cared for the two human babies. We have modern stories of children who were supposedly raised by some wild animal. We have the famous fictional story by E.R. Burroughs of "Tarzan of the Apes."

The Instinct to Nurture creatures of a different species is not limited to the nurturing provided by humans to other creatures or of other creatures providing nurturing to humans, but is also found within other quite dissimilar species who at times are willing to provide nurturing in the form of food and protection to the infant creatures of a species which is markedly different from their own kind. There are unusual occurrences of nurturing, which testifies to the instinct's powerful ability to conquer all synthetic barriers between different species, such as a bird that provides food and protection for an abandoned kitten, a mother cat that willingly allows a puppy to suckle her milk, a mother dog who suckles a kitten, and the list of those unusual kinds of extra-species nurturing is long and amazing and provides us with yet another example of Mother Nature's multifaceted incomprehensible schemes for survival and clear evidence that her instincts are deeply and powerfully embedded within many very different creatures.

The Instinct to Nurture is surely, in terms of its contributions to our kind's survival, one of the most significant of all instincts, and it is probably the primary instinct, which eventually directed our kind to undertake the work of domesticating animals and plants, a task that was with the most certainty initially instigated by women within whom this instinct is found to be most powerfully expressed.

The instinct to suck is an instinct that is incorporated within the basic nature of many creatures other than just mammals. In mammals and particularly in humans, the instinct to suck, like other instincts, is one that lasts for a lifetime. The sucking reflex instinct first develops within the human embryo during its earliest fetal stage, just as soon as the developing nerves can establish a functional connection to the fetus's developing muscles that are used to perform the sucking instinct.

Small children even after the time they have finished nursing for mother's milk like to have a pacifier to satisfy this instinct. If pressures from various herds did not condemn this instinct, it would be the normal situation to find some kind of pacifiers in common use within the adult human population. Many times individuals who have the strongest inclination for this instinct are thumb suckers even after they have become adults. Since thumb sucking is essentially condemned by the mythology of some herds, those individual adults who perform thumb sucking, usually automatically resort to it only during sleep or during very private times. Adults many times resort to instinctive sucking rituals during various sexual activities that take place in private places, and they consider these actions as very adult and separate from the more primitive Instinct to Suck, when in fact they are not separate. The Instinctive desire to suck is so basic and so much in need of some regular satisfaction that many persons find joy beyond the sweetness and flavorings of hard candies in the sucking actions that are usually used to consume these types of candies. **The Instinct to Suck is such a benign instinct, and yet it gives so much personal sensual pleasure that people should regularly satisfy its desire.**

The Instinct to Groom is common to many very diverse creatures ranging from the birds to our family of primates. When two creatures engage in grooming and being groomed they are indicating to each other at a most primitive emotional level that they both accept each other within the bonding of their social structure as friends or minimally as not being enemies. For Primates, including humans, grooming is a method by which they can accurately determine which individuals within their group are really their friends as compared to those individuals who are falsely professing to be their friends. Those individuals who are in fact an enemy are loathsome about coming into any kind of contact with the body of their enemy. And they will make it a point not to get involved in any kind of grooming situation with their enemy, simply because being in such close proximity of your enemy as is required to engage in mutual grooming is potentially a dangerous position to be in, and could result in immediate physical harm. In some rare situations there are always some few individuals who believe they might cleverly deceive an enemy, by performing grooming, into believing they are actually their friend. But the sensual relationships involved in grooming are so ancient, primitive, and beyond mere conscious realizations, that what transpires between the one who is grooming and the one who is being groomed is a primitive kind of sensual communication of bodily touch, whose language can hide no lies about real feelings or real intentions. This language is so powerful in its direct truthful sensual communication that it communicates the untarnished truth about the true motives of the individual who is performing the grooming. Considering this at a more personal level, if your enemy is brave enough to try to fool you into believing that they are your friend, and they are willing to touch you, then you can feel within the nature of their touch, that they do not like you, and that they are actually repulsed by coming into contact with your body. You can discern by the nature of someone's grooming touch, exactly, precisely, how they feel about you. And of course it is also true that how and where you allow the one who grooms you, to touch you, conveys volumes of information to them about exactly how you feel about them. **Touch is the most powerful form of instinctive truthful communication between individuals. It is so basic, so primitive,**

and so ancient in its origins that the lies of a spoken language cannot tarnish or hide its revealed truths.

Our kind has a primitive instinctual love of the softness of fur. When as a child we had our first experience of touching a soft fury animal, an instinctive knowing of this ancient primitive sensory pleasure comes immediately into their mind, and their thoughts are taken mysteriously and instantly back in time to their instinctive remembrance of the warmth and security that the feeling of touching soft fur represented. We should reasonably suppose that at sometime during our distant past, we were creatures who were covered with warm soft fur and because of this we have come to instinctively recognize the feel of soft fur as a primary ancient characteristic of our kind, and whose soft furry feel activates a nebulous instinctive memory of some distant and long lost ancestral mother. It would seem that the warm feel of soft fur and its association with our distant ancestral mother's milk have somehow become instinctively entwined.

Because of the powerful and pleasurable instinctive memories we associate with the feel of fur, we should at every appropriate opportunity choose to ware soft furs as part of our clothing accessories, but since it is not now our own body's fur, we should use synthetic man made furs for this purpose, and not the fury skins taken from animals. There is no excuse that can justify the further use of animal skins to adorn our furless bodies. Synthetic furs can be made that are incomparably better in their structure, softness, and exquisite pattern designs than are any animal furs.

The Instinct to Build is strangely common throughout much of the animal kingdom, and we should realize that this is so because of the great survival advantages it gives to the creatures that build nests or other homes. Having a specialized nest or home, which protects creatures from the elements of weather and from those other creatures, which seek them out as food, is a primary contributor to their survival. The structures animals build range from the simplest burrowing structures, to complex nests of all kinds made from grass, twigs, branches, mud, saliva, gravel and many other mediums. This same Instinct to Build is the prime mover in humans, which eventually has led us into constructing the towering buildings, homes, roads and other structures that are constructed by our kind. This Instinct is really most amazing, when we consider the very complex structures that are produced by the different creatures that exhibit this instinct. Creatures other than humans are able to build marvelously complex structures that fit their specific needs to near perfection. This is an instinct that bears true testimony to the nearly unbelievable complexity of the mechanisms of instinct and to the astonishing results, which instincts can deliver.

The instinct to bring food from the place it was obtained to a more secure environment has surely had important benefits for all those creatures that exhibit this instinct, including humans. You can observe even today, that those wild creatures who attempt to consume the food that they have obtained without first bring it to a safer place often have their meals stolen from them by some fiercer creature. The simple act of bring food to the surroundings of the home provides two very important ingredients for survival. Firstly, a large friendly group can then protect the food and secondly it allows for the sharing of the food among the members of the group, and in this way the instinct substantially contributes to the inter-bonding between members of the food-sharing group. We could believe that the sharing of food within a common group is the primary force for strongly bonding with other members of the group, and is, an even more powerful mechanism for bonding than are sexual relationships between the members of the group. Sexual relations, between the group's members, are probably the second most important element in establishing strong bonding between the group's individuals.

Subconsciously we must realize the great importance, in the bonding between individuals within the group of the family and or friends, which is played by get-togethers where food is consumed within the safety of the home. In more distant times, this sharing of food within the tribal group was certainly the single most important method of unifying the group for working together towards common goals. In today's world it is sometimes difficult for families to share this still most important ritual for bonding. The single most important ritual for establishing and maintaining strong bonds between the members of a family or groups of friends is the sharing of food within a safe environment. It is an ancient ritual that surely precedes even our kind's becoming human. To not honor this instinctual force, weakens nature's basic fabric that binds relationships. This instinct is one that should be honored at every possible opportunity.

In humans, and to some degree in other mammals, there exists an unusual instinct, the Sympathetic Instinct, whose strength or weakness of expression seems to vary ever so slightly from one individual to another until the full spectrum of its possible intensities has been represented within the population. An individual's degree of sensitivity to having a sympathetic reaction to the emotional state of another individual is a result of instinctive mechanisms, which are exhibited from the time of a person's birth. Sometimes this instinct is so powerfully represented in a child that the parents often can see its intensity even in their very young children. We can sometimes see the Sympathetic Instinct being exhibited by mammals that are quite different from humans. These mammals usually exhibit the Sympathetic Instinct by showing their sympathy for other individuals of their own kind, who have suffered physical wounds or death. These creatures display their sympathy by using body language actions that unambiguously communicate their sympathetic meaning to their own kind and are powerful enough to communicate their meaning across the barriers that separate species. Their clear signs of sympathy are obvious and touching, and are strong enough visual and or vocal patterns to evoke a sympathetic understanding in humans.

Within the extremes of this instinct in the human population are those individuals, who are so sensitive to the emotional state of other persons that we might name them, **"Sympathetic Resonators."** These are persons, whose extreme sensitivity causes them to actually feel in reality and within their own bodies the emotional experience that another person is feeling. They can actually feel within themselves, the physical conditions of pain or joy that they detect are present within another person.

At the opposite end of the intensity's spectrum for sympathetic responses are those individuals, who have no sympathy at all for the emotional state of another individual. We might call such persons, **"Sympathetic Duds."** These are persons who are unable in anyway to empathize with the emotional condition of another individual of their own species or of any other species. These "Sympathetic Duds," if they should happen by accident or by design to cause physical or emotional suffering to another individual, they are unable to feel any remorse either for their actions or for the sufferings of the other individual. Luckily most people in the general population lie within the bounds of these two extremes of intensities for the expression of the Sympathetic Instinct and most persons exhibit a mid-range of sympathetic reactions to the emotional state of other creatures.

The Sympathetic Instinct surely is an element that springs from the sense that individuals within a group are emotionally bonded. In the truest sense it is an instinct that strives to be a kind of self-protection, where an individual is able to see within others a part of their own image of self. Surely this instinct has been an important contributor to both the survival of groups within a species and also therefore survival for the individuals that exhibit this Instinct.

COMMON ACROSS SPECIES INSTINCTS

We usually think of sleeping as something we consciously decide to undertake. For most persons, who perform regular and routine daily schedules, have significant mental stimulations, and some minimal physical activities, after they have decided to retire for sleeping, sleep comes to them relatively easy. We normally do not think of sleeping as an instinctive condition, and the reason for this is because we usually retire for sleeping long before the Instinct to Sleep attempts to force the sleeping state upon us. The Instinct to Sleep is so strong when it becomes activated, that if we are to then remain awake, we must make monumental efforts to stay off sleep. We should come to understand that the driving power behind the Instinct to Sleep is the brain's attempt to shut down all of the different sources of sensory information coming into our short-term memories, simply because our short-term memories have somehow become over-burdened, over filled, from storing of all of the day's sensory and emotional happenings. The sleep instinct's powerful attempt to shut down the sensory inputs to our brain's short-term memories by means of sleeping is the way we are able to become temporarily isolated from our real time sensing of the objects and events within our environment and the day's emotional memories which we have self generated. During the time we are sleeping, our remembrances of the day's happenings, which have been stored within our short-term memories, are compared, sifted, and sorted by the brain's mechanisms for dreaming. Our periodic dreaming during the time we are sleeping clears away the day's memories from our short-term memories and moves those memories which are significant for us to remember into storage within our long term memories, and in doing so, in moving the memories, a dream is created whose content consists of a series of events, the initial event or image of our visual dream is always a memory from the short-term memory which is being moved from the short term memory to be stored within the long term memory. The succeeding events of the dream's unfolding imagery come from those other memories within our long term memories that have long been resident there and are in some way associated to the dream's initial causative memory. Sleep with its dreaming that carefully sorts and unloads the short-term memories is most likely a creature's way of protecting their long term memories from a potentially disastrous overflow of unsorted, irrelevant, and chaotic information that exists within the real world.

Sometimes while driving an automobile the Instinct to Sleep becomes so over powering that it cannot be resisted. If at these times the automobile driver will stop and sleep for only ten or twenty minutes, the dreaming that takes place during sleep will bring relief by diminishing the contents of their short-term memory, and even this minimal amount of sleep and dreaming will be sufficient to shut down the Instinct to Sleep and the driver can then continue with their driving. If the driver attempts to use stimulants such as caffeine instead of relieving the storage burdens of their short-term memories and by this means continues driving, when the stimulants finally wear off, the Instinct to Sleep will return with more powerful demands for sleep than were present before the stimulants was consumed. The only reasonable and natural solution for shutting off the Instinct to Sleep is to in fact sleep, and thereby allow the short-term memories to be relieved of their memory burdens.

It is believable that our kind's first means of communication with one another was certainly by means of body language. Communication by the means of merely assuming a certain pose of the body, or by simple or complex movements of the body, is certainly the most primitive form for communicating our desires or our intentions. Body language can sometimes be the most effective way of communicating our mental state of mind. More elaborate body language signs can communicate by means of such simple gestures as, finger pointing to indicate something of interest, and signaling with the hands can indicate for someone to go away, stop, or come to us. The hands can be used to form approximating shapes that are rudimentary symbols that can represent the dominant features of some animal. Such hand signals can be used while silently hunting animals as a source of food, or to give a silent warning of the presence of an animal that is dangerous and should be avoided. In our present time, we can see that symbols that can be formed by the hand can be representative of our complex written and spoken language. It is believable that our most ancient direct ancestors had a great wealth of hand formed symbols that could quite satisfactorily communicate the needs of their life styles. Although the use of our hands to form symbols is not in itself instinctive, such a complex way of communicating surely grew out of the natural simple hand gestures that do seem to be instinctive as they have been common to our kind throughout time.

We see in our primate cousins the chimpanzees, when they are in a group of their kind, and they are suddenly and joyously surprised, they instinctively jump up and down, while waving their arms in the air above their head and screaming unintelligible vocalizations. And we see within our own kind this very same Instinctive Body Language reaction to a moment of sudden joyous surprise.

Throughout the different creatures within the family of mammals, including our own kind, we observe the bowing down or the assuming of a prostrate position as an across species body language symbol, which indicates sexual submission. Usually this kind of signaling from a socially lower ranked individual, to a more dominant animal, is the signal from the lower ranking animal of its willingness to be sexually submissive. The sexual submission signaling is not usually acted upon, but is ceremoniously and ritually acknowledged by the dominant animal, when he assumes the mock position for initiating the sexual act, but does not proceed beyond the mere assuming of the position. We humans are still willing to bow and/or prostrate ourselves before some symbols and costumes that are supposed to represent a dominant power, and most persons would not think of relating these body language signs back to their real meaning as seen within the rest of the animal kingdom.

The origins of different body language symbols or signs, one of the most primitive means of communicating, must lie in our most distant past. And because of the long time separation between the origins of this instinct and our presence in the modern world, it is very difficult to even detect or understand all of the ramifications that body language has for our own kind, but surely there are a great many, and some of them must be of a continuing consequence to our everyday life although we may be totally unaware of them and how they surely influence our interactions with other persons. Most of us have experienced the situation where upon being introduce to a person we have not before met, a person who is new to us, we immediately discover, for some reason that we cannot quite put our finger on, that we simply, and in a most general way, do not like the person. It seems apparent that the newly introduced person must have exhibited some body language communication that we found as unacceptable. Most likely neither of the two persons cognitively understand what has happened in such a situation. Sometimes the dislike is a shared mutual feeling, a symptom of clashing subtle body language signs.

Throughout every part of the animal kingdom, we can see creatures that make complicated or subtle movements of their bodies to communicate with their own kind or with totally different creatures. Many times the most beautiful and complex body motions exhibited by some birds are directed towards obtaining sexual favors. While watching the very complex mating dances of some birds, we might find it difficult to believe that such a very complex sequential string of muscle controlling patterns, whose causative neural signaling is being issued from their birdbrain, could be hereditary. But, we are quite willing to believe that the equally complex physical designs and color patterns of a bird's plumage are inherited and we know from the controlled breeding of birds that the complexities of plumage are without doubt a hereditary condition. Being reasonable persons, we must then also be biased into believing that the most complex of instinctual body movements are also necessarily hereditary.

There are certainly body language patterns that can communicate between species. The intent of the crouching position that predators, including humans, take when sneaking up on their pray, is easily understood by most creatures. Also the mere lifting of the arm as if to claw or strike is a body language sign that communicates easily between species. The sudden up lifting of the arms with the fingers of the hands spread to symbolize claws, and sometimes accompanied with a growling sound, is commonly used as a means for humans to frighten each other.

When you have known some person for enough time, you usually come to know some characteristic features of their body movements, features that are unique to them. In general, we all move our bodies in very common generalized patterns of movement, which are dictated by the structures of our muscles and bones, but written upon these generalized movements are very subtle variations of movement, instinctive movements, which define our own movements from those of other persons. Because these instinctive movements are imposed upon and within the general body movements of our species, we can see the truth of their inheritance. When we see some grandchild, who has never seen or in anyway been exposed to their grandfather, and we can sometimes plainly see the signature of the grandfather's body movements written in the movements of the grandchild.

There are many body language expressions, which the facial muscles can subtilely write on the human face, expressions that can communicate with great accuracy numerous different emotional conditions of our being. And many of these instinctive facial expressions are also expressions that are common to our relatives, the chimpanzees. Our facial expressions are usually directly tied to our immediate emotional state of mind and we physically express our emotions by smiling, frowning, laughing, or crying. Faces instinctively and automatically express our surprise or feelings of shame, guilt, remorse, or uneasiness and anxiety. Just the very slightest movement of a facial muscle or movement of the eyes can present an entirely different emotional mood than that which was before expressed. There are static facial states that are important clues about an individual's physical health.

There is a problem in not being able to identify all of the instinctive body language communications that are common to our kind and also those that are common to other species. Realizing that reactions to body language signs can be instinctive and powerful, understanding them can only be to our great advantage. Consider the situation we often times hear, when some human in dealing with a different creature, a creature from the wild, a creature who has been their long time friend, and then, for no apparent reason the human is suddenly and without warning fiercely attacked and sometimes killed. There is certainly the possibility that the human inadvertently made some body language sign, a sign whose meaning was unknown to the human, yet it was a sign that was so powerful as to trigger the "Savage Instinct" within the wild creature, which consequently led to the injury or death of their long time human friend. We might wonder about the situation where some breeds of domesticated dogs, which are known to be sometimes vicious, are prone in certain situations to attack a person. It is certainly a possibility that some persons, when they are confronted in anyway by a dog, they inadvertently and unknowingly present some body language sign or signs to the dog, which instinctively causes the dog to instigate, as the dog's self defense strategy, an attack against the person.

Much of the overall nature of all animals is their instinctive reactions that assist in their survival. Therefore, a major component of these instinctive reactions might be associated with sexual activity. We should be willing to consider that body language, which is of a most primitive origin, must have many signals that are concerned with communicating sexual interest, desire, willingness, or rejection. These body language signals might also be able to communicate the magnitude associated with each of these feelings. **The most emotionally powerful connections, understandings, which can be made between two people, are those that are communicated solely by body language.** There are no written or spoken languages that can compete with the mystic ancient primitive power of body language. For human males an erect penis is a clear body language sign, which is signaling, yes, yes for a sexual encounter, even though their spoken words might be falsely claiming the opposite. **There is the distinct possibility that some sexual body language signals are too strong to be overridden by spoken language symbols. A situation could arise when a spoken "No" is overridden by a more powerful body language signal that is strongly saying "Yes." Herein, we can see a further need to understand what Body Language Instincts are all about.**

The hoarding of material goods is an instinct that is common across a broad spectrum of species. It is even present in insects like ants and bees. We see it exhibited by birds, and by squirrels, but it is most highly developed and exhibited by humans. In some persons the instinct is so powerful that they hoard every kind of physical object, and are mentally unable to part company with any of them. In other persons, it is exhibited by the hoarding of certain selective types of objects and we kindly refer to those persons as "Collectors" instead of hoarders. In many persons the hoarding is specifically oriented towards those items that might be required for a comfortable long-term survival. Usually the primary items in this group are money and/or food. The Instinct to Hoard is the mother of the emotion that is displayed as greed. The Instinct to Hoard has served us well through difficult times, and generally serves us well at the present time.

Within the framework of deeds that surround the **Instinct to Persecute** as a means to escape from being persecuted are some of humankind's most regrettable injustices. The mechanics that underlie this instinct start as weak and simple seeds, which can easily be recognized as detrimental and evil, and at this point in the instinct's beginning realization, it could be quickly and easily shattered and thereby stop its further development into the full-grown terror that it can finally become. What nourishes this instinct during its early awakening is fearful silence. This instinct almost always starts as a seed in one individual, or within very small group of individuals, who begin the persecution of an individual or a small group of individuals. The persecutors discover that they are generally unopposed in their persecutions, and so then other members of the society join in with them and they join with them simply out of a fear, that by not actually belong to the group of persecutors; that those persecutors might somehow see them as being in silent opposition. Given time the ranks of those who are the persecutors grow more-and-more in numbers by the simple mechanism of the fear that if you are not one with the persecutors, then you might be identified as a de facto member of the persecuted group. The momentum of this instinct can grow until the persecuting group has become a major social herd, and all nonmembers are so fearful of the herd that they remain silent even when they see the persecutor's herd committing the most inhumane injustices. You can witness this instinct's beginning signs of awakening, and its attempt to survive on any primary school yard within the world, or within some economically disadvantaged minority groups where individuals are hard pressed to meet the needs for their survival within an otherwise opulent society. If this instinct's awakening is not summarily stopped at its infant beginnings, it surely becomes a full-grown monster of injustice, which is then difficult or impossible to stop because of the great number persons who make up its ranks.

You can also witness this instinct's basic flowering and functioning in a yard of domesticated chickens where its consequences can quickly become bloody, and one of the chickens is pecked to death by a mob of their sisters and brothers.

There is only one hope of stopping the cruel injustices, which this instinct to persecute always brings, and that is to stop it at its very beginning, otherwise fear will become its powerful shield and its mechanism for growth and survival.

For some creatures, an important part of their instinctive nature is to lie. This does seem to be the case for humans. Lying clearly has specific advantages that aid a creature's tactics for survival. To be able to deceive another creature, or even your own kind, is a most basic means of escaping from a situation that might lead to severe consequences. Lying naturally exists at almost every level of the animal and plant kingdom. Lying can involve the physical presentation of certain fixed visual patterns, which are otherwise naturally exhibited by an entirely different creature. Lying can involve the release of chemical patterns that drift through the air or water and convey a lie about the identity of the individual that originated them. In nature there is pretty much a set of lies, which are appropriate for confusing one or many of the senses of another creature. For humans, lying is sometimes committed by deceptively using certain body muscles, which is lying by using body language. So called con-men are wonderfully proficient at lying by their use of body language, and it is probably this, more than the words that they speak, which instinctively lures their victims in to their con. Facial expressions are many times used in conjunction with a spoken lie as a means of trying to lend the lie some additional credibility. A faked direction of movement is a kind of lie in common use among creatures to momentarily throw their opponent off balance. **But, lying as exercised within the human population reaches its summit and its crowning glory by the use of our written and spoken languages.**

Common among many creatures is the Instinct to Steal another creature's prize or their belongings. In humans, items of theft include both physical and intellectual property. Usually after a creature has made its theft, it flees to a place of safety, their nest or home, where their new acquisition can be safeguarded from others who might attempt to take it away from them. For most of the creatures of nature, stealing is mainly directed at the theft of food, but it can also involve the stealing of another's nest, burrow, or some other kind of home. When the stolen prize is food the grab it and flee technique is most commonly used to safely escape with the prize and humans oftentimes use this simple method of escaping from the place of their theft. There are those persons in whom the Instinct to Steal is so powerfully controlling they are unable to resist its unreasonable desires. We have named these persons "Kleptomaniacs." In human populations every imaginable kind of physical item and even intellectual properties are subject to being stolen. Human history is filled with examples, where an individual's original creative intellectual prize has been stolen, and then the creative origin is attributed to the thief and the rewards eventually come to the thief, while the real originator of the idea is left with neither credit nor rewards. It was not until very recent times that laws have been written in an attempt to protect the creative originator of an idea from those who freely make use of their uncontrollable Instinct to Steal. But these laws, which are meant to protect against the theft of intellectual property, are most times circumvented by clever legal strategies, which involve in one way or another, the degradation of idea's originator and legally contrived long drawn out delays in bring the case before a court of justice. Theft within human societies is rampant. The Instinct to Steal first raises to recognition in small children, who feel free to steal at their slightest urge. Society is at a loss for being able to control this instinct, simply because it is so prevalent within the population and its actions span the entire range of human endeavor. **The best that any society has ever been able to accomplish at controlling the Instinct to Steal is to severely punish those persons who are caught at stealing outrageously large quantities or outrageously high valued objects. But while the few are forcibly deterred from stealing, the multitudes fulfill their Instinct to Steal by the theft of millions-upon-millions of small innocuous treasures, and these thieves usually escape from any significant notice of their individual small crimes.**

Some of the most often mentioned of all instincts, which are common to nearly every animal from the simplest creatures to the most complex creatures are the instincts which cause a creature to either fight or flee from a situation that subjectively seems to be life threatening. Although these instincts are commonly found as generally identifiable reactions within most all animals, the range of the intensity of sensory stimulations, which can trigger the fight or flee reaction, varies over a very broad range for the different families of creatures. Also the intensity of these instinct's reactions varies greatly for different families of creatures. Even within the same families of animals, including humans, the intensity of stimulation, which will trigger the fight or flee instincts and the reaction at being triggered, has a wide variability from one individual to another. For humans both the triggering level for these instincts and the reaction's intensity after being triggered is dependent upon an individual's initial ambient state of their emotions and of their alertness. In some individuals, who are either paranoid or are on the borderline of being paranoid, the Flee Instinct is always in a delicate balance for being triggered by sensory situations that to more stable individuals would not ever be noticed as threatening in anyway.

Both the flight and flee instincts are readily observable in young children. A young child if they feel they have been offended will instinctively physically strike at their offender. Or if their offender appears as too threatening, they will retreat to the safety of a parent's arms. Children are prone to demonstrate their automatic instinct to fight, to strike, particularly when the object that causes their offence is some inanimate object, such as one of their toys. It is a completely natural situation for children to use physical force against those things, animate or inanimate, which offends their sense of dominance over their world, but it is essential that parents, other care givers, and teachers educate the children to control their temper in situations where they believe they have been offended. We too often see within the world of adults some of those persons, who were never strongly disciplined, when they were young children, to control their instinctive reaction to strike at persons or objects that have caused them some minor offence. If during childhood and young adulthood the instinct to fight is not conditionally modified to appropriately fit the instinct's triggering event, then those adults whose instinct is totally uninhibited will cause great problems for society.

SEXUAL INSTINCTS

SEX

The elements, which make up the sexual instincts, are potentially such powerful thought directing and controlling forces that when they become fully activated they can dominate a creature's every thought while relentlessly and tenaciously ever driving the creature towards obtaining sexual satisfaction. Realizing the potentially uncontrollable power of the human instinctual sex drive, societies have contrived various clever means of channeling, diverting, and minimizing its free expression.

Just how do most all societies, which are powerfully influenced by their various dominant religions, approach sex and the multitude of different ways of naturally expressing the divers drives associated with the sexual instincts? They ban certain kinds of acts, from the multitude of sexual acts that can bring us great pleasure, along with the accompanying physical and mental bonding which is a primary part of the mystical ritual of sex, and given enough time, they will soon enough, have some kind of religious taboo attached to each of the most stimulating acts for obtaining sexual satisfaction. When religions have enough power, they will surely leave us with only one religiously acceptable sexual act, and that of course bears the name of its simple minded founders, "The Missionary Position." It would seem that only god knows, as is commonly said, how many different possibilities there are for having stimulating joyful sex, but if you let religion, or a government influenced by religion, to condemn on any grounds one of the sexual possibilities, then you are opening up the door for a religion to next decide that maybe your way of enjoying sex is to become the next unholy no—no, and then you will be the one to be persecuted, not by god, but by an ignorant arrogant and nearly logically blind religious society. Some religions now see even the most basic and fundamental sexual performance, which is needed for the reproduction of our kind as a dirty necessity, which our bodies must perform to the disgust of our observant holy spirit. The religiously inspired social sexual taboos are contrived in an attempt to turn us all into righteous sexaphobics.

There can be little doubt that within the animal kingdom, the nature of each creature's sex and sexuality are determined by factors of heredity. But whereas both the physical and mental characteristics relating to an individual's sexuality are determined by heredity, the nature of the physical and mental aspects of an individual's sexuality are not necessarily the same.

The instincts involved in sexual attraction are highly driven by hereditary pre-programmed visual and auditory filters, which our different senses use to tell us something about the overall condition of the person we are momentarily considering and about some very specific features of their body. The appearance of the hips, waist, buttock and breast are very important instinctive sexual stimulators. The image of a face being symmetrical has a great importance in determining sexual desirability. When the facial image is symmetrical it is seen as beautiful. It has been suggested that regular symmetry of the face and head is an indication that the individual's head and what is inside of the head is genetically all right.

In general, when one is visually determining the sexual desirability of some potential partner, there always takes place a quick visual scanning of the potential partner's overall body. If the body looks generally symmetrical, it is a powerful indication that it was derived from a good and complete set of inheritable genetic instructions. In most of the cultures of the world, clothing inconveniently hides most a of a person's body from being directly viewed, but humans are powerfully adept at visually interpolating exactly how the body hidden beneath the clothing would appear if it was directly revealed. And it is oftentimes the case that the body that is imagined to exist beneath the clothing can be more sexually exiting than if the actual hidden body was itself revealed. The style of clothing in some cultures is particularly designed to successfully hide the non-erect and erect size of a male's penis. The non-erect size of a male's penis has a primitive and powerful influence, as to where other persons within the society believe he should be placed within the social ranking, and the larger the penis, the higher on the scale of primitive social ranking the individual is imaginatively placed. By using various methods for keeping the size of a male's penis unknown, other factors than penis size are able to vive at establishing a person's social ranking with the social structure This most primitive part of the sexual instincts, the mystical power embodied within the size of the penis, is possibly one of the main reasons why nude beaches and other areas for nudity are usually completely forbidden, few and far between, and when they are allowed some minimal existence, they are restricted from the view of the general public

Since the sexual instinct is truly older than the hills, "instinctive sexual desirability," as rated by nature's sexual instinct, is all about a symmetric and strong muscular or plump physical body, which is what Mother Nature rates as **"Prime Meat"** in her rules concerning what it takes for simply surviving in a vicious world. Truthfully in the world of instinctive sexual desirability, there is no natural sexual attraction for the intellectual abilities of a potential mate. Be cognizant that here we are talking about sex, sexual desire, and the instincts, which drive two sexual partners together and to then engage in having sex. **These sexual instincts have nothing whatsoever to say about choosing or about directing us towards a partner, which might result in any kind of long lasting compatible and stable relationship,** a relationship where the partner's intellectual and emotional characteristics, and not their physical characteristics are the primary long term stabilizing elements which bind two people together in a compatible and mutually satisfying long term relationship. The "Sexual Instincts" are all about bringing the mating partners together and then getting down to having sex, and nothing else. In our present societies, we allow the sexual instincts to overcome and to override our intellect, and to more or less willingly allow our sexual instincts to drag us into marriages, which were primarily based on the powerful forces of instinctive sexual attraction, and this attraction standing alone as the sole binding force of the marriage, gives the marriage little chance of happily surviving the ever revealing winds of time.

Both men and woman look for the physical determinative sexual indicators within each other. If all of the correct physical parts are signaling sexual attraction, but some body movement tells a negative story, or there is discovered some physical damage, or there is some appearance of sickness, or some weakness, then all of the sense of sexual attraction can be immediately canceled.

Since the sexual instincts consist of some of the most powerfully dominating instincts, and since they are very much about establishing an unusually strong attraction towards the observable physical characteristics of a potential mate, we should guess that sexual attraction is also affected by the potential mate's display of their body language. Consider the very strong emotional bonds that most all children establish with their parents, independent of whether the parents of the child are, or are not, their biological parents. We must suspect, as is sometimes said, that when choosing a mate, a male looks to find a mate that in some ways resembles his mother, and a female looks to find a mate that in some ways resembles their father, let's call this phenomenon the "Father-Mother-Attraction Axiom". As concerns two mated persons, we can, by simply observing their dominant physical characteristics, often see that this Father-Mother-Attraction Axiom seems quite often to be true. But if we could also see the common body language relationships that might exist between the mated persons and their parents, we might again discover, that in this way, the Father-Mother-Attraction Axiom has again been validated. We can never be entirely sure, as to what physical and body language characteristics of a parent, are those most strongly and indelibly written into a child's memory, and are for the child, the primary identifying factors that represent their parents. But, when we are considering the mother's and father's characteristics that make up the bonding image which is indelibly written into a child's mind, the image is necessarily one which was formed very early in the child's lifetime. So it is this earliest image of their parents that the grown child looks to find within their potential mate. If we could know these factors, I'm sure we would then be able to more clearly see that the Father-Mother-Attraction Axiom is a major final factor in the choosing of a mate. It is, as if Mother Nature is saying, "This combination worked well before, so let's try it again."

It is probably a good bet that one result of the Father-Mother-Attraction Axiom gives rise to the phenomenon that is usually named **"Love at First Sight"** or **"Instant Love."** This of course is a real psychological condition, which happens in the natural world of both humans and some other animals. It is a nearly emotionally over powering experience and the truth behind this love at first sight is that it is the Father-Mother-Attraction Axiom being realized to its most powerful extent and therefore it is actually a kind of love at second sight. It is an emotional condition, which is brought about by unknowingly detecting the primal elements of the Father-Mother-Attraction Axiom within the person with whom you fall in love with at first sight. It is such an over whelming emotional experience that the person who is the object of love is seen as the most attractive, beautiful, and completely most irresistible person that could ever be imagined. Its emotional spell of desire to have that person cannot ever be compared as equivalent to the common every day finding of a person of the type to whom you are usually sexually attracted. Those encounters where two persons meet and they experience this phenomenon of **love at first** sight are most certainly destine to be happily bonded together for their entire lifetime.

It is sadly true, within most societies throughout the world that they attempt to forcefully warp sexual attraction into social and legally binding contracts of marriage. In a more distant time of our past, such binding contracts where about nurturing and protecting the offspring, which in those days would be the inevitable result of most sexual relationships. Today, there are those persons aboard their hypocritical battleships, who seem to be ignorant of the powers of Mother Nature's sexual instincts, and they bombard society with slogans about sexual abstinence, just as if once the cork is coming out of the bottle of champagne it can be indefinitely stopped at the bottle's lip. The driving forces of the sexual instincts are so powerful, that in almost every case they flood over and smother the necessarily weaker and less powerful commitments to abstinence. And in those few exceptional cases where a commitment to sexual abstinence is able to survive, its survival can in almost every case be attributed to a naturally occurring diminished sex drive that is ever present within those individuals who are successful in maintaining their commitment to sexual abstinence.

Our societies are so deeply plagued with religion's multitudes of sexual no-nos and taboos that our natural sexual instincts have been so warped, contorted, and forcefully unnaturally transmuted, that our peoples are totally confused about the real meanings of romance, sex, love, and long term personal relationships. Sex should never be used as the sole driving force behind marriage, or for any other long-term personal bonding. When two persons share together a long-term personal sexual relationship it is a most powerful method of establishing a mutual mental bonding. If the sexual relationship is continued for good length of time, the bonding between the two individuals becomes so strong they each feel in some ways, that they are at lease in an emotional sense a real part of each other. They feel in a mystical sense that they have become partially bonded together as if they were one person, and if either of the two is in anyway verbally or physically attacked by another person, then the attack is seen by the non-attacked partner as a direct attack upon their own person, and their response to the attacker can clearly be seen to be representative of this feeling of oneness with their sexual partner. Some animals other than humans who pair together with a sexual mate, and where the pairing lasts for a lifetime, often demonstrate even more powerfully than do humans their feeling of oneness and they are tenacious at protecting their mate to the point of sacrificing their own life. This powerful part of the sexual instinct, which can naturally give rise to a mental bonding which manifests itself as a mentality of oneness, is identical to the non-sexual bonding of some parents with their offspring, which is not uncommon throughout much of the animal kingdom and is often demonstrated by the parent's willingness to fight to their own death to protect their offspring, who are mentally seen as one with the parent.

A very strange abnormal situation exists in our so-called modern world. We live in a world were the religious authorities and their conditioned puppets of power, a long with their brain washed public supporters are absolutely rabid in every respect about any sexual relationships, which are not about producing children. These people are also nearly thrown in a spastic frenzy, should they discover that a child has seen or heard of any kind of material of a sexual nature. Have any of these self-proclaimed sexual control police ever taken a good look at the natural world of the other animals. You can clearly see within the natural world that the Great Creator God has displayed there for all to view absolutely every kind of sexual behavior that could possibly be imagined, and there is no natural censoring curtain that can be drawn over what takes place there, the real Great Creator God sees absolutely nothing there, which requires being either censored or in anyway hidden from anyone. It is the very nature of the sex acts of every kind that there are no naturally occurring taboos associated with any of them. And there are no sexual acts of any kind, as long as they are entered into voluntarily and are not associated with pain or other purposefully imposed mental sufferings, which are detrimental to the participants in any way, and certainly do not result in any short or long term detrimental physical or psychological effects to the individuals. In nature's natural uncorrupted world, sex as it naturally flows from the intricacies of the sexual instinct is driven, by instinctive curiosities, towards every possibility of sexual discovery and experimentation. It is only in society's unnatural world of conjured up sexual no-nos and taboos, which are drummed day and night into our brains that psychological hurt can fallow certain sexual relationships, and these hurts are solely able to thrive and survive, because the individual who carries them within their thoughts has been sufficiently brain washed and indoctrinated, so that they make their own mental suffering in response to how they have been taught about how they should be suffering because they have experienced one of the many taboo forbidden sexual encounters. Every period of history clearly without even the slightest doubt needs to have its equivalent witches, its conjured up sinners, its victims to burn at some righteous stake to set a stern warning and as means for inducing fear into the general population's mind. Our time's equivalent witches are those persons who partake of some kind of sex, which is forbidden by laws that were instigated primarily as a result of some religious sexual taboos. Those persons who violate these unnatural laws and taboos, when apprehended are sacrificed to a suffering which is beyond any falsely believed hurt they have caused, and whose only hurt within a victimless but so called victim's mind is all of the making of a very unnatural segment of our so-called righteous religious society, which has diligently and fitfully worked at unnaturally poisoning our mind against certain kinds of sexual encounters.

The days are hopefully long gone when every sexual encounter necessarily produces a child. If society is to ever be truly psychologically healthy, then sex must have its open place in societies, and hopefully become as natural a pleasure as is any of the other of nature's wonderful sensual pleasures. Persons living within a mentally healthy society should have a place of safety, where they can visit and share a sexual experience based on mutually acceptable terms of the sexual participants. For any society to condemn and to discourage sexual activities between sexually mature individuals inevitably leads to the opening of a Pandora's box from where emerges upon society a nightmare of the most horrible and unbelievable of sex crimes; all stemming from repressed sexual desires which are then satisfied, by sexually tormented individuals, upon unwilling partners. And these kinds of forced sex acts, perpetrated upon unwilling partners, are so prevalent within today's societies that they should stand as a logical condemnation of the unnatural sexual taboos, which are their primal cause and brought them in the first instance into existence. Sexual relationships that do not produce children should not have any place on anyone's philosophical radar screen.

Mother Nature's prime interest in heterosexual relationships is her concern to get the female's egg or eggs fertilized at any cost. In Mother Nature's relentless drive to get the egg fertilized, she was forced into selecting a system of unequal desires and unequal sexual performance between the two sexual components, male and female. Natural selection has necessarily selected for males who are able to perform the sexual act and to quickly have an ejaculation with its accompanying satisfying orgasm as the signature that their sexual function has been fulfilled. On the other hand, natural selection has necessarily selected for those females who were much slower than males in being able to obtain sexual satisfaction during the time of sexual intercourse, and also in selecting for females who are unable to ever have a sexual orgasm during the time of normal sexual intercourse. There are some women who will freely admit that it is difficult or impossible for them to have an orgasm during sexual intercourse, but it is sure, if the truth were known, that many, many more women than now admit to this situation, would also have to admit to it.

The seemingly unfair difference in the time it takes for males and females to reach a state of sexual satisfaction during sexual intercourse is a prime contributor to the survival of our kind, and to the survival of the other creatures of nature who sexually reproduce.

These seemingly unfair natural differences are absolutely necessary as a means of guaranteeing the female's egg has the best chance of being fertilized, because if the female was naturally able to reach a satisfying orgasm during sexual intercourse before the male experienced an orgasm, she would likely push the male away as soon as she had been sensually satisfied, and this situation would not allow her egg to become fertilized. By Mother Nature selecting for the disparity in the time it takes the male and female partners to gain some sexual satisfaction, nature has chosen a method that gives the best possibility for the female's egg to become fertilized during sexual intercourse. Sadly for the females of the modern world, we find that because of nature's natural selection, that most females are unable to have a sexual orgasm during the time it takes for a male to perform his part of sexual intercourse and to reach his satisfying sexual climax. There are many females, and probably all of them, who are unable to have a sexual orgasm by any means, and there are also some males whose anatomy is complete, but who are also unable to experience a sexual orgasm from any means of sexual stimulation. Therefore in modern times, where the production of children is most often of a secondary concern in sex, and where mutual joyful pleasure is the primary concern, then for both the male and female partners to have a mutually satisfying sexual encounter, it should be considered that sexual means, other than sexual intercourse, might offer a better possibility for realizing some kind of mutual sexual satisfaction. Male partners need to be educated that sexual intercourse might be a curse for their female partners in not being able to achieve sexual satisfaction, and that other methods might prove to be more satisfying for both partners.

It's a cruel trick that Mother Nature has laid upon the females, but its results have been very successful for the survival of each species.

No one can say with absolute certainty that any women can actually have an orgasm in a like manner as is had by males. It seems that the physical mechanisms necessary to produce an orgasm are simply missing in a women's anatomy. In our present time where females are struggling for their equal place in all aspects within a world that has previously been dominated by males, it was only natural that females should lay claim to their equality in the previously exclusive world of a male's sexual satisfaction through male orgasm. Many women of today are unwilling to bow down to any proclaimed differences between the two sexes. And so the idea of a female orgasm equal in every way to that had by males soon took root and gained in popularity and even spread to the so-called sex specialists of the medical community. It is nearly unthinkable that anyone should now days question the truth of the sexual equality of the female orgasm, which is professed as a reality. We might see how ridiculous is this demand that all things between the two sexes must be equal, consider if males, not wanting to seem lesser in any respect than females, began claiming that they are in fact equal to women in every respect, and they are fully capable of having babies, but they are doing it secretly, off and away from were the truth of the matter can be seen. Surely the males are here faking it, but then?

If we would like some supporting evidence to better decide about this female orgasm controversy, we might find it in other members of creation, particularly among those creatures that do not have a complex spoken language with which they can say what is true, verses what they physically demonstrate is true. Let's look at the female mammals and discern if they do, or do not, have sexual orgasms during their sexual intercourse. We can look to the mammals other than our kind and see what their natural actions can tell us in truth about this matter. The other mammals cannot by means of a spoken language lie to us about their sexual activities. We can see the truth of this matter in how the females behave within a sexually active group in their natural environment. We see the females, in a sense, are only waving their asses in the air, when they are in heat and are in need of having their egg or eggs fertilized. And when they are not in heat, they are uninterested in any sexual activity with any male. We should believe that if female mammals had a sexual orgasm during sexual intercourse, as male mammals do, then females would also be very interest in having sex regularly and frequently even when they are not in heat, as males are always interested in sex. Males, knowing in reality the pleasure of the sexual orgasm, are very much interested in experiencing another orgasm at nearly any and every opportunity.

If Mother Nature had endowed females with the ability to have a sexual orgasm during sexual intercourse, then it must somehow or in someway be shown how this necessarily contributed to the survival of the species. If this cannot be clearly shown, then it is quite certain that nature never gave this "Orgasm" reaction to females. And if it is argued that the female orgasm is a kind of vestigial function, then it should clearly be stated, what lost but necessary functional sexual gap was importantly filled by it in the distant past, and whatever function a female orgasm might have purportedly filled must be shown to be an important contributor to our survival, as is the male's orgasm. Evolution has developed the male orgasm as the means to very powerfully indicate to the male that his part in sexual reproduction has been completely accomplished.

It is of the utmost importance that females only seek or attract males to engage in sexual intercourse, when they are chemically primed to ovulate and get their egg or eggs fertilized. If females were always willing to engage in sex, even at times when they were not primed to have their eggs fertilized, then they would seriously be depleting the fertility of the population's males by encouraging them to expend their sperm in an attempt to fertilize, un-fertilizable females and such a seeking of sex by un-fertilizable females would in the truest sense deplete the normally strong urge within males to have sex at every possibility and decrease the probability of fertilizing a needy female.

When females are resistive to having sexual intercourse until the time they are fertile, they essentially ration out their sexual favors, thus making this commodity relatively scarce to the world of males where it is always in high demand. In the societies of the civilized world, women have long been accustomed to the male's desire to seek out and find sexual satisfaction wherever they might come upon it. It is as natural for the males of all mammal species, including humans, to seek out a great number of different sexual partners, as it is natural for most birds to fly. And so it has become a ritual of the human female's cult to pass down, from mother to daughter, from sister to sister, and from one female friend to another, their understanding about their natural desire to only allow sexual intercourse with males when their female body's chemistry signals that they are ready to be fertilized, and that they might tend to be somewhat nasty, unapproachable, and ornery with males, when they are not prepared to have their eggs fertilized.

The passed down cunning rules of the cult of women at every opportunity uses every means possible to keep men close to them, even during the times the females are not feeling sexually receptive, and by numerous deceptive means **"to have"** men, or a man, in their continual presence; so that the males are there and available for the time the female does become ripe. The basic reason behind women's use of facial cosmetics is to falsely advertise, that they are in estrus and are ready to engage in a sexual relationship, this they accomplish by means of coloring some of their facial features, which makes them appear more radiant as if they were truly in estrus. In today's world in has become very popular for the females to synthetically enlarge their breast to enormous sizes as a false indication that they are sexually primed to be fertilized when in fact they are not. It is the general case that women use every means they can contrive to indicate to the males that they are always ready for sex when in fact they are not ready, at least not in Mother Nature's definition of being ready. But unlike most all of the other male creatures of nature, the human male is totally oblivious to these contrived false female's signals and follows and sexually hungers after any sign that in anyway seems to advertise that sex might be readily at hand.

Men instinctively and nearly uncontrollably contribute their own means of falsely marking an individual as being sexually ripe and ready. It is men who, when they are in a close association with males or females, simply and instinctively cannot resist the urge to slap an associate on the ass. Of course this in more primitive times was a means of making a person's ass red as a false indication that they were ripe and ready for sex. We often see this instinctive automatic and irresistible slap on the ass taking place between members of sport teams, but there its implied meaning has been degraded by time to only being a sign of friendly acceptance without usually being associated with any sexual connotations.

Understandably in essentially every society throughout history, women have been overly ready to fulfill the needs of men other than just their sexual needs.

And we see in most every society that it is the women who essentially perform the nurturing, grooming, maintaining of a comfortable home environment, caring for the offspring, preparing, cooking, and serving food, and all of those service functions that are usually provided by a good partner in any functional symbiotic relationship. And it is by the performing of these service duties that women have in the past historically equated these acts of service as a counter balancing weight for their lack of interest in providing sexual pleasures for their mates during the times their own emotional basic nature is not interested in having sex.

Society, at least subconsciously, for time immemorial has understood the sexual situation of the females, and because of this, the society has realized the need to keep males in a close proximity to females even when the female is not ready to be fertilized, and has seen fit to provide even stronger bonds by means of the institution of marriage, which attempts to lock the male to the female, and to forbid the male or female from seeking any kind of sexual satisfaction which lies outside of the bonds of marriage. It is the case that many religions, although not exactly understanding their own reasons or motives have command their women to be obedient to their husband, meaning by this to satisfy their husband's sexual needs even though the women might not be naturally in the mood for having sex. Marriage seems to be instinctively outside of the natural mental condition of males. In many species, males can be seen to be actively seeking sexual stimulation at every opportunity, when there is not present some other higher instinctive priority, which represents a more primal need than is the male's instinctual drive for sexual satisfaction, such as the need to eat to satisfy a demanding hunger, or the instinct that commands the male to fight to protect themselves from impending death, or the instinct which causes them to flee from a escapable dangerous situation. Other than these three instincts, which are of a higher priority than are the sexual instincts, when these three instincts are not in demand of needing to be satisfied, then the sexual instinct drives the male to be searching for some opportunity to obtain some kind of sexual stimulation. It seems to also be part of the general nature of males to soon loose sexual interest in any individual partner and to seek out whenever possible new individuals for sharing a sexual relationship, but the male does not in most cases abandon their original sexual partner, this is probably as a means of having an insurance policy for guaranteeing there is a fallback choice for sexual stimulation. When it comes to sex, most males are pretty much ready for anything that will give them sexual pleasure. And counter to the male's sexual nature of instinctively free roaming, it seems to be the general nature of the females to be monogamous, as a means of guaranteeing the safety of their offspring and the sanctuary of the home.

It can't be denied that women can experience some kind of emotional reaction to some sexual stimulation other than at those times she is in heat. And it would seem that these emotional reactions can be lasting and satisfying, but they are not the equivalent of a male's orgasm. In this respect some women say that they can have multitudes of orgasms during sexual intercourse, but if these purported orgasms were in any way equivalent to the orgasm that males experience, then it is sure that such women would require intensive long term hospital care as a means of recovering from the series of powerful impacts to their emotional psyche. If a male experienced multitudes of orgasms during sexual intercourse, he would be physically unable to move, and would need to be confined to his bed until he was able to emotionally recover from such an overpowering physical and emotional experience. So there are clearly some disparities between what some women report about their orgasms, and what is physiologically believable, and also what is believable as is evidenced within other female mammals, who all seem to go about sex as a kind of rather boring necessity and not as any great thing of sensual pleasure.

I hope you are now wondering, if most women, and possibly all women, are not having a sexual orgasm during sexual intercourse, in the same manner that males can physically and mentally experience an orgasm, then what is it that so powerfully attracts women into strongly desiring and engaging in sexual acts. The truth of this matter is that the forces of sexual desire are not in the first instance about obtaining an orgasm. Those first demanding and all powerful forces of attraction, which drive our kind into first desiring close intimate physical contact with another individual, and which very soon can lead to the sexual act, are nature's instinctive desire, as it is sometimes said, **"To Have"** the person of our desire. This powerful drive **to have** the person of our instinctive desire is common in initializing the sexual act for both women and men. This part of the sexual instincts, **to have,** is much about driving us into a situation that results in providing proof of our mutual acceptance of each other. The fact that the inevitable result of this situation, our powerful desire **to have** another person in our physical possession, and which eventually can lead to sexual intercourse or some other sexual act that results in an orgasm is a mere secondary consequence of the initial driving force. This, **"desire to have,"** is a part of the sexual instincts that is the ethereal substance of the physical and mental aspects of desire, romance, love, and friendships. Real love is actually about this initial driving force of the sexual instincts, the desire to have, to be near to, to become a spiritual part of another person. Many persons, both men and women, are driven by this desire to have an other person, and they are sometimes quite willing and driven by strong desires to satisfy another person, sexually, or other wise, without any concern for themselves finding any physical sexual satisfaction in the experience, but they instead find a satisfaction of equal merit in the fulfilling of their desire **"To Have."** This part of the sexual instincts, **"the drive to have,"** gives us the desire for physical contact, to be in the neighborhood of those we desire, to dream and think of those whom we desire. This "To Have" part of the sexual instincts is common to most of the more advanced creatures of nature and is surely what can draw females temporarily into close contact with males, who are interested in pursuing more that just closeness. It is clear that in many creatures during the time the female is in estrus, their **"to have,"** desires are so heightened, they use every means at advertising their desires to be both accommodating and close, and to be **"had."** But this is not directly about their desire to satisfy something sexual, it is merely Mother Nature's trap that makes a sexual relationship possible and probable. We see within the human population some women and men are so driven by the need **to have**, that they are unable to control their desire. It must be a common situation for those persons in society who become the stalkers of others.

Most persons who are healthy, sexually active, and have ready access to a sexual partner, often resort to satisfying some of their sexual desires by performing masturbation. Private masturbation allows an individual to engage in using substances or sometimes devices, which they would most likely be too self-conscious to use in the presence of another person. Masturbating in private also gives an opportunity to contrive all kinds of personal mental sexual fantasies, which for various reasons they are unwilling to share with other persons, including their usual sexual partner or close friends. The individual who masturbates in private can call to mind visual images that are the ones, which are the most sexually stimulating for them. They often recall images from their sexual past that are about some of their most exciting and enjoyable sexual experiences. Sometimes they fantasize about their desire to engage in a sexual experience, which they strongly desire to have, but have been unwilling to fulfill because of powerful threatening social taboos against realizing it in reality.

Each of us is born with a predetermined sexual preference, which certainly is determined by hereditary factors. It does not take much investigation to understand that individuals, from their earliest years, have strong feelings concerning the direction of their sexual orientation. They did not have to be schooled to know it. They did not have to be brainwashed to know it. Their sexual orientation was upon them naturally from the time of their earliest feelings for others within their species. It is quite clear from listening to many individual testimonies that whatever a person's sexual orientation might be, that it was there as a natural condition of their being, and that it remains constantly the same and unchanged throughout their lifetime as does any inherited trait.

When we consider sexual preference for persons of the same sex, we come upon some rather unusual circumstances. If we are thoughtful, we are forced to wonder about the genetic nature of this instinct. It would seem highly unusual if its source was genetic in nature, since in present society it is commonly believed that members of this group do not reproduce themselves. It is an undeniable fact of nature that if a kind does not reproduce itself, then eventually its kind dies and becomes extinct. Also, you simply do not get elephants by breading rabbits. If in fact, you should like to believe that this trait, this instinct, is not inherited, then you are faced with a miracle in nature that is equivalent to a virgin birth.

Careful consideration might leads us to believe, that because of the extreme pressures of the "Herd," many in this group are socially forced into acting against their real sexual preference for their same sex. And because of the nearly unbearable pressures from the dominant social herds, they feel forced into a heterosexual marriage, where they also feel obligated to produce children. In our society to have children is generally considered as the triumphal and undeniable proof of the parent's heterosexuality. By means of an essentially herd forced marriage, and its resulting children the genes for this sexual instinct are passed on to some of their offspring. This seems the most reasonable and understandable way for this particular sexual instinctive trait to have survived throughout all of recorded time, and it is an instinctive trait that is found within other creatures within the natural world.

It would seem the most logical assumption, that sexual preference is instinctive in essentially all cases.

This then must lead us to some further unusual speculations. Within the general population estimates for the percentages of the population that profess to a sexual preference for the same sex is in a low percentage range of around five to ten percent. I believe that based on the assumption that this instinct is most likely an inherited instinct, we have to consider that it exists in a much larger percentage of the population. Just considering the proportions of a normal bell curve, and that many within this sexual preference group are forced by society's herd pressures to disavow their natural sexual preference instinct, then we can be very suspicious of the usually reported numbers. It is more likely true, that somewhere near 5% are in manner, as this whole group is characterized, and it is somewhat easy, by merely observing their body language, to identify those members of the group. Just keeping in mind the normal bell curve as applied to this group, but speaking of percentages as applied to the overall general population, it is reasonable to believe that there is another five percent, who are members of this group, but are mannered like alpha males or alpha females, and they simply exist in society totally unsuspected of their real sexual preference. We are still left to consider those persons represented at the middle of the curve. At the middle of the curve some ten to fifteen percent must lie somewhere between the two extremes at the ends of the curve, and they necessarily must have discernable characteristics that are a moderation of those more extreme characteristics represented at the two ends of the curve. Those in the middle of the curve surely have traits that are relatively indiscernible from fully heterosexual individuals. We should also keep in mind that those in the middle of the curve have characteristics and inclinations that span between homosexuality and heterosexuality. We might reasonably suppose that if the general population was not inhibited by the unnatural condemnations of the herd, that as many as fifty percent of the population might be willing to freely express, and happily engage in bisexual behavior, which they do not see as an unnatural behavior. Within the population, of the middle and upper curve percentages, most persons who are part of this group are surely married persons and most of them surely have children, a fact that might be reflected in-part by the high divorce rate and the serious unhappiness among those who stay married, either because of duty to their children or for other less noble reasons, such as their financial situation. Many of those who stay married certainly have a life with some happiness, but it must be certain, because of the most powerful nature of this sexual instinctive drive, they must have a chronic feeling of dissatisfaction with their situation, and of their life being in some way unfulfilled. Based on these considerations we might be suspicious of the reasons for the high rate of suicide among teenagers. It is sad to note that the teenage suicide rate appears to be the highest in those areas of the nation where religious influence is most dominant, and where religious intolerance against this group is the strongest.

Within the over-all population of those whose sexual orientation is directed towards their same sex, there are those persons who feel driven to hide their true feelings simply because of the nearly overwhelming condemnation, which comes from various herds and their associations with institutionalized religions. There are therefore many homosexuals who remain hidden within society, and as a means of camouflage, they use the age-old adage that "The best defense is a powerful offense." They therefore try to hide their own instinctive sexual nature, by waging a vengeful and unforgiving war against their own kind. Sigmund Freud pointed out this very situation. Not being open about their own same sex preference, they usually hide behind some mythical righteous fortress from where they hurl their insults and condemnations against their own kind.

Any non-bigoted and serious religious scholar of the unholy holy books will tell you, that just because something has been written there, it does not mean that it is the word of any god. The unholy holy books are collections of somewhat historical writings, written by men, and as such those men had their own personal and social axes to grind. During the period of history that the unholy holy books span, any sexual act that did not result in the bearing of children had to be absolutely forbidden. Each tribe's survival was dependent on their women producing the greatest numbers of children, simply as a means of trying to balance out a nature that took them as a sacrifice to their time's gods of ignorance. In ancient times, an average mother was lucky to have just two or three of her children survive to the time of their sexual maturity. To encourage the family to "Be fruitful and multiply" and to damn any and every sexual activity that did not produce children was a tribe's, a city's, and a nation's main philosophy for survival, and not just surviving, but also to grow in its numbers and therefore in their world, which was absolutely dominated by religious herds, to grow in power.

Even a casual examination, of societies and their culture's throughout history, indicates conclusively that there does not exist any natural instinctive bias against homosexuality. It is clear that all biases against members of this group are perpetrated by various "Institutions of the Herds" that feel they have something special to gain for themselves by condemning members of this group. And what it is—they feel they gain—is babies—many, many, many new babies, who are destine to become the new members of their religious herd.

It is quite understandable why Mother Nature has never produced any instinctual biases against homosexuality, and it is simply because those who are male members of this group do not generally engage in the competition with the other males for female reproductive mates, and so there is no reason for the heterosexual males to be biased against them. And, dominant heterosexual males have always systematically raped those members of the group, who are physically female.

We can often see in the boldest of unequivocal terms, how some members of dominant herds are willing to demonstrate their obvious ignorance and their own hypocrisy by persecuting members of their herd who are discovered to be homosexuals. We have seen, all too often, when some soldier has been greatly honored for their exceptional positive contributions to their military organization, and then at some later date it is discovered that the same soldier is a homosexual, then instantly, the military organization withdraws their already given honors, and labels the soldier as an undesirable person and discharges them from the military organization. There are those within our military organizations who don't mind publicly displaying their irrational, illogical, and hypocritical way of thinking, it is those persons who should be publicly dishonored and discharged from their military service, and if those same persons were ever to command our beloved young soldiers in a combat situation, then pray to every god to save our soldiers from their kind of illogical thinking. The military services should, by all good logic, be pleased and overjoyed at having within their organizations, homosexuals who desire to militarily serve their country. Why? Because all homosexuals, who live within our loving, caring, forgiving, so called religious society, have by the time they are eighteen years of age, already survived eighteen years of a kind of extended "Boot Camp" that was for them, a social hell, a hell where it is physically and psychologically more difficult for an individual to survive, than to survive in any military boot camp. They survived our religious society's social boot camp of hell, which a stupid, ignorant, and intolerant falsely professed religious society has forced them to endure as just a part of their growing up.

At least for males the combination of the nearly irresistible powers of the sexual instincts, which are constantly driving them to seek out sexual satisfaction, and the counter balancing powers of the social sexual taboos which are forbidding sexual freedoms, between and because of these two opposing forces a most striking and unusual situation sometimes arises. Sometimes there are groups of males who are brought together in some kind of free and natural association, a group of friends, a club whose members share common nonsexual interests, and over a period of time it comes to pass that nearly everyone within the group is having some kind of sexual relationship with nearly every other person within the group. But each individual member of the group believes that they are the only one who is having sexual relationships with the other members, and because of the influence of the strong social taboos each individual strictly keeps the knowledge of their sexual affairs to themselves. It comes to the situation that nearly every member of the group is having a sexual affair with nearly every other member of the group and the whole interwoven relationship is completely and successfully hidden from the individual group members and to any persons who are outside of the group. So-called professional sex surveys are never able to uncover the interwoven sexual goings on within these unusual groups, simply because the taboos which forbid such sexual intricacies are strong enough to lock their individual knowledge in a secrecy that is even more powerful than are the taboos that caused the knowledge in its first instance to be locked within the individual's memory. If there was time, thirty or more years, to carefully build up a strong and trusting relationship with some of the members of these groups, then the interwoven sexual relationships might be discovered by putting together the various individually supplied pieces of this not so unusual but marvelous secret sexual puzzle.

Yes, certainly there are many sexual situations whose intricate hidden natures will never be discovered and disclosed, simply because some of the social anti-sex taboos will so powerfully forever lock the only knowledge of them within the individual participant's minds.

The time may not be too far off before we might be able to identify the specific genes, which coupled with potentially non-inheritable genetic changes might determine the instinct for sexual preference. I believe it would be the gravest error, if we tried to vary the gene structure of any individual to change their same sex preference to opposite sex preference. Mother Nature has, in her own time-tested wisdom, somehow given us this instinctive same sex preference. It surely is there for a good purpose, even if we in our ignorance do not exactly understand. As a society by meddling with this instinct, we could suffer a major loss of creative talent. Human history bears witness to the greatly disproportionate high number of meaningful contributions made by individual members of this group. They have been some of the world's greatest political leaders, military leaders, philosophers, teachers, scientists, artist and athletes. It certainly seems that coupled with this instinct, is a different way of seeing and understanding the world, and because of it, society has been privileged to receive insights and other contributions from the members of this group, that others rarely find. Any society, which nourishes their community of homosexuals to flourish in safety, always wins with their honoring of diversity, a great advantage of insight and creativity, which significantly contributes to new discoveries in every field. We need to, at every opportunity, stand up against those near-sighted fools, who without logic or any good reasoning attempt to condemn members of this group, as the members of this group are one of the most valuable human resources that any nation can ever hope to have working for a better future for all of its people.

Independent of sex and sexual preferences, the time is long overdue, when societies should consider other opportunities, which can provide even stronger stabilizing social elements, than those ideas that are from the distant past and are still being forced down our throats as the necessary and only social elements that can stably bind society together. A much more powerful philosophy, which is ever-more capable of commonly binding society into a more individually satisfying and a more functional social group, is to be had by simply recognizing that persons of the same sex generally find they have more common understandings and are more emotionally suited to living with each other, than they are suited to living with their opposite sex, and they daily gain a greater satisfaction from living with their own sex, independent of whether they share sexual pleasures or not. Persons of the same sex who like each other and who get along well together, because they share common interests, usually discover that their life together becomes both emotionally comfortable and pleasant, which is something more than can be said of the situation within many marriages and many families. Society needs to change away from those stringent inflexible ideas about what cements the social fabric and yet results in so much unhappiness within the social fabric. Society needs to promote and honor personal linkings, which give the individuals the best possibilities to be creatively productive and to better seek out their own happiness.

PATTERN INSTINCTS

Our instincts that are associated with simple and complex static patterns, which exist in nature, are in many cases obvious, but surely there are many that have not been recognized. It is interesting that for the most simple of these Pattern Instincts, we can see many of what are essentially the same instincts exhibited in creatures that are of an entirely different species.

Here I will list only a few instincts as a means of giving a cursory idea about them, as most everyone has some familiarity with them:

There is an Instinct that attracts us to objects in the natural world that are shiny, and to other objects that are unusually colored as compared to the general background color. The general nature of this instinct is that we are attracted to anything that is an inflection point (a point of noticeable difference) as compared to the general color or luster of the environment that surrounds it. We see this instinct is common in many creatures other than humans; birds and even some insects exhibit this instinct. It is certainly an instinct that has directly contributed to our making many valuable discoveries; quite obviously it led to our discovery of the naturally occurring shiny metals, and also to many of the brightly colored compounds of other metals. More basically this instinct draws our attention to the unusually bright colors of fruits and nuts that lie somewhat hidden and buried within the foliage of some plants.

We are instinctively attracted into investigating objects of all kinds that show a regularity to their structure, including uncomplicated geometric objects, straight lines, perpendicular lines, triangles, squares, rectangles, and circles, etc. It is not unreasonable to believe that this instinct has strong connections to our inherited Visual Alphabet of Patterns and to other of the most basic structures within the brain, which are involved in the brain's pattern coding in preparation for pattern information's storage into memory.

We are also drawn instinctively to investigate other more complicated but regular geometries, particularly the three dimensional geometry's of inorganic crystals and the regular organic geometries that are the immediate representation of all living things.

We are instinctively drawn to investigate, with some reluctance, holes. Curiosity about the whole range of holes seems to be on our instinctive menu, little holes, large holes, and even dark holes are a sweet attraction. It is not difficult to imagine how well this instinct has served us through the ages.

Just as speculation, we might consider that there may be multitudes of simple visual static patterns, which to us as Homo sapiens and to other creatures instinctively communicate information that is of a great importance for survival, patterns that upon their detection, rise up great fears, or beckon us towards safety, or call to us powerfully in some unknown way.

Here we have so far considered a very few of the static visual patterns which are instinctive triggers. We of course realize that patterns detectable by each of the other senses must necessarily have many instinctive reactions associated with them.

The Sense of Smell detects patterns that represent chemical agents that are drifting in the air, in the water, or are resident in the ground. We are beginning to understand in detail just how very important the Sense of Smell is at instinctively controlling the actions of many of nature's creatures. We might assume that it has powerful affects on our own kind.

An instinct associated with the Sense of Taste, and is known to everyone, was surely a powerful influence in contributing to our survival. This is the instinctive scowl that spreads across a human's face at the taste of anything that is particularly bitter. Even the smallest children exhibit this instinct. The scowl is a powerful nonverbal body language warning to others that the substance is not desirable. Bitter taste is the common across species warning sign that a substance is poisonous.

The detection of sounds especially those sounds that we associate with music are a kind of moving pattern. They exist as tonal conditions that flow through time. We have a strong attraction to those tonal qualities that in their atomic form make a pattern whose structure exhibits a gracefully extended regularity in time. These patterns in time are sounds, such as the sound produced by the vibration of a string, or the tones produced by wind instruments. We are also instinctively attracted to those sounds in nature, which are repeated singular patterns, such as the regular pecking of a woodpecker, or the regular beat produced by a percussion instrument. We can only guess at some of the reasons behind our clearly instinctual attraction to musical sounds. It might be, as suggested by others, associated to our bonding with the rhythmic sound of our mother's heart beat. I suggest that our attraction to musical sounds probably also has much to do, with the sounds produced by those other creatures of nature, whose vocalizations were never indicators of any kind of threat to our kind, and whose communicative chorus was a kind of song to our ears, which meant to us that all was safe and well within the near vicinity. The natural sounds made when normally still water is being disturbed, are for all creature's ears a music of attraction that draws our interest and curious attention, like the night moth that is instinctively drawn to the light of a flame. When the naturally wonderful sound of the chimes and tinkling of water meets our ears our attention is drawn to the sound as surely as to any mythical siren's call, and we cannot escape our attention to it. Even if we drift into sleep, the sound of the water's music still dances in our brains as a signing that its balm of goodness is at hand. Water is such an important element for life's survival that all creatures of the land, which require it in abundance are instinctive drawn to its music of motion and its life-giving promise.

We also realize, that most of the sounds produced by musical instruments are powerfully representative of the sounds that are common within the human voice, whose tonal qualities can touch our emotions in many different ways. When we listen to any piece of music, we travel on a quite an unusual mental journey. It is a most unusual journey as compared to most journeys. When our sense of sight is taking a journey through the patterns of the visual landscape, we can in a sense, see into the future. As we physically travel along, we can see distant objects and watch as they slowly come closer-and-closer. As those first distant objects draw ever nearer, they reveal more and more the details of their structure. On the other hand, a musical journey is like traveling or moving, when you are facing backwards to the direction of your movement in time. You cannot detect any musical sounds in the future, because they have not yet been born. At every instant in time, each and every note within the musical journey is suddenly, as if from nowhere, born fresh and new. Their sound image, their musical structure appears instantaneously and develops to its fullness like some phoenix arising from nothingness. The sound images construct their evolving forms within your memory, and they slowly fade into the receding landscape of sounds, where their structures dim and disappear in time, at the same time ever-new tonal patterns are born instant-to-instant as the musical journey continues. It is often said that "A picture is worth a thousand words", but for the human ear, a piece of music is a thousand dynamically mutating pictures for the ear, all made from glorious sounds.

We should give some thought to the fact that the very nature of the audio elements of sound, which are primarily characterized by their frequencies and varying intensities are directly analogous to the frequencies of the natural nerve impulses which bring the sensory information from each of the body's senses into the brain. But for all of the senses, other than hearing, there does not exist an exact one to one, kind on kind, relationship between what the senses have detected and the frequencies of the nerve impulses, which bring the information to the brain. The taste of strawberries does not by itself have a frequency, which represents it. The smell of a rose does not have by itself a frequency that represents it, but a single audio tone, or the sound of music, whose frequencies are detected by the ear are represented in kind by nerve frequencies that are transmitted to the brain. It is maybe because of this unusual one to one, kind on kind, frequency to frequency, similarity between an audio frequency's sounds and how they are conveyed by similar nerve frequencies to the brain that makes sounds, particularly musical sounds, so emotionally attractive to the listener. It is as if the audio frequencies from the natural world are able to communicate unchanged directly with the audio structures of the brain.

Patterns represented as a shadow that suddenly appears above the head of a creature brings a sudden instinctive alertness. And, any pattern that moves unexpectedly in our peripheral vision also brings to us a sudden instinctive alertness. Here you might think back to consider the instincts of the Frog and realize that this same instinct is common to both humans and Frogs, although when we are startled by a moving shadow within our peripheral vision, we do not hop off towards the darkest non-moving part of our environment.

Any visual or sound pattern that appears too suddenly and strongly automatically causes our body to instantly recoil.

GENERAL BODY
FUNCTIONS

Most, and probably all body functions exhibited by living creatures are totally instinctive in their basic causative nature. The well-known examples are: The constant and regular beating of the heart, and the natural repetitive breathing of air. The reflex system, which automatically initiates salivation when certain food substances are either seen, tasted, or whose aroma has been sensed in the air. The reflex system that allows us to automatically swallow food or other objects that have been directed into our throat, and of course the associated reflex systems of the stomach and guts in their work of moving and digesting food. There is an instinctive system, which allows warm-blooded animals to regulate their body's temperature. We all know of the instinctive reflex systems, which indicate the need to urinate and/or defecate and which accomplish these tasks. There is the rather strange instinctive reflex which causes us to desire to urinate when we hear the sound of running water, this instinct might have had its origin back in the times, when we as an individual within a small herd performed mutual and simultaneous urinations as a means of heavily marking our group's territory. There are many animals that instinctively defecate and/or urinate as a means of marking out their territories. Then there is the instinctive reflex that can cause the automatic regurgitation of the contents of the stomach when the body has somehow sensed the stomach's contents are undesirable, and there is also the instinctive automatic regurgitation that can usually be induced by simply moving a foreign object across the back-wall of the throat. There is also the very gentle repeated instinctive reflex which causes our eyelids to blink as a means of distributing the eye's tear over the surface of the eyeball; this reflex also comes into automatic play whenever the visual system detects an object which is quickly moving towards the eye. It is instinctive to like the taste of sweetness and to dislike the taste of bitterness. It is instinctive to seek the comfort of warmth when we are too cold, and to seek coolness when we are too hot. There is the instinct, common to many creatures, to automatically scratch their itches.

The instinct to "Yawn" and to make some sound while yawning is most likely the vestigial remains of an instinct, now nearly lost in our remote past, from a time when our distant ancestors exhibited this instinct in a more powerful form, then, like it is for the wolves of today, it was probably a call to all of our kind who were within hearing distance to respond with a similar call. It is observably true that when an individual's yawn is accompanied with the sound usual to yawning, it more powerfully invokes an automatic response of a yawn from those persons who are nearby and hear the sound.

There is an instinct, which is common within the kingdom of animals, for creatures to clean their extremities and face after they have eaten. Even human children, who are not notable for self-cleaning, become upset whenever their hands become too sticky, and they desire to clean away the stickiness.

Throughout the animal kingdom, creatures are born with the instinctive ability to move their body. Each creature, including humans, is born with separate individual instinctive mechanisms, which control the general movement of each of their body's muscles. It is by this means that even infants are able to make those body movements that we can see are of a most general nature and have not yet been tuned towards fulfilling any very specific functions, other than to defecate, urinate, or eat which in mammals is exhibited by a coordinated use of their mouth, tongue, and throat muscles all used to produce a powerful clamping and sucking rhythm. The instinctive muscle control mechanisms to be able to perform exacting controlled actions must be modified and refined by means of intelligent learning, which makes use of the sensory inputs to monitor and modify the movements.

Some animals are born with a highly developed Instinct to Move. Some animals within hours of their birth exhibit body movements, which are essentially equivalent to the controlled body movements of their kind's adult population. Animals, who at the time of their birth demonstrate a highly developed instinctive ability to control their muscular movements, are able to further refine those inherited body movements until they have been finely tuned, to meet their exact needs for surviving in their particular natural environment. For some animals, including humans, the Instinct to Move shows itself to be both extremely generalized and weak at controlling body movements at the time of their birth. We can witness the weakness for control of body movements in the nearly uncontrolled flailing of a human baby's arms and legs. Those creatures who are born with a highly developed, in terms of control, body movement instincts are representative of one end of the spectrum of this instinct, while humans are representative of the other end of this instinct's spectrum of inherited muscular control. Nature shows us that those, in which this instinct is most highly developed at birth, are greatly limited in their ability to further extend the complexity of their body movements much beyond those at the time of their birth. A tiger will never be seen playing a piano, walking a tightrope, ice skating, or dancing a ballet, but their body movements are superbly and expertly adapted for their needs in the wild. On the other hand, humans learn to modify and control their body's movements to include an almost unbelievable wide range of extraordinary movements. Almost every movement of a human's extremities are learned moves, and this includes the most simple movements such as reaching out with the hand to touch an object that is within sight, to the nearly miraculous movements of a human's fingers and hands as is demonstrated in the playing of a musical instrument. Some humans learn to so finely tune the control of their body's movements, that by this means as a species humans can move more precisely and exquisitely than any other creatures within nature's creation.

The instinct, which causes us to suddenly and automatically withdraw any from a source of pain or irritation, is certainly one of the most useful and most primitive of all instincts and is common to all creatures right down to some bacteria. There are other instinctive motor reflex systems, which cause the automatic contraction of certain muscles when their associated reflex nerve is stimulated by being bumped or touched.

When we are hungry, the instinct to find food and to eat is common throughout the animal kingdom. For humans who live in societies where there is an overly abundant supply of food, we find that there are many people who regularly eat far more food than is required to maintain their body's need for immediate consumable energy and so the excess intake of food is stored by the body so it might be used during times when environmental food sources are scarce or missing. But why is it that so many people regularly over eat, the real reason is both simple and obvious, and that reason is, that eating is a hundred times more satisfying and enjoyable than ever is the best sexual experience, and for this reason alone, people are driven to eat, eat, and eat. Mother Nature has designed the sensual rewards derived from eating to be the most rewarding of all of a creature's sensual experiences, simple because the body's intake of food and drink is the primary means by which all life is sustainable. All of the next in importance of a creature's survival instincts "fight or flee," and even the sexual instincts are subservient to the instinct for a creature to eat. The sexual instincts and the sensual rewards associated with its fulfillment might seem to be the most enjoyable during the transitory time of the sensory sexual climax, but in reality they are orders of magnitude lesser than the long lasting enjoyment that can be obtained from eating delicious foods, and the extended enjoyment of eating can be experienced many times during each day. So we are doomed, by the priority which Mother Nature has placed on us for consuming food, to being ever drawn to eating and therefore to the consequences of excess body weight which result from our over eating.

THE INSTINCTS OF RANK

Within our kind and also common to most other creatures, is an instinctive reaction against magnified individual diversity, and so we look upon highly noticeable physical or mental deviations from those characteristics we feel are the norms of the herd's members as undesirable characteristics. This instinct functioned in our kind's prehistoric past as a powerful means of recognizing and eliminating those individuals from the herd's hereditary gene pool of any individuals whose genes might be detrimental to the herd's continued survival. In the ancient selective blind ignorance of Mother Nature's stumbling to preserve the true and tested creatures, this instinctive reaction against magnified individual diversity tended to serve well its purpose. And because of this instinctive bias against extreme diversity, only those individual's whose physical or mental characteristics where just slightly different from those of the general population, where the individual differences that were able to slip through the fingers of this kind of sorting and sifting instinct. A certain consequence of this instinct's functioning is the very slow but generally steady course of the evolution of all creatures. And so to our detriment in today's societies, this instinctive bias against those individuals who exhibit any magnified difference of character, are singled out and are subject to being persecuted, solely because of their very noticeable differences. In modern times, if the members of the herd are not restricted from acting against the individual who is seen as different, the members of the herd will by all available means attempt to force the different individual to the bottom of the herd's social pecking order. If the herd's members are totally unrestrained in the possible actions they might take against the different individual, the herd's dominant members will proceed by means of physical force to possibly kill and destroy the individual. For children who have not been taught to accept individual differences, even minor differences such as some child's allergy is seen by other children as a clear reason to view the child as substantially different and then the herd begins its torment as a means of pushing the child into being seen as undesirable, and as an outsider to those within the common group of the herd. This instinct is so primitive in its origins and the reasons for its functioning, that it coupled with some other equally and out-of-time instincts are the primary cause of many of societies seemingly uncontrollable crimes of violence which stem from those instinct's automatically spawned unhealthy hatreds. This instinct needs to be recognized for its primitive unacceptable nature. We must forever work by every means at subduing its continued haunting of society's best hopes for peace and the sanctity of the individual. In today's world allowing this primitive instinctive kind of selection of who should survive and who should not survive, would be a disastrous philosophy for society in general, and understandably it is usually squelched and dealt with quite severely in most civilized societies, yet it is an instinct and it is forever able to survive within some people with all of its sadistic powers intact.

For many of the more complex creatures of nature, there is a well-established instinct that exists within the individual members of a herd. It is an instinct, which drives the herd's individual members to establish among themselves some ranking of their position within the hierarchy of the herd. This ranking of an individual's position within a group is referred to, as their "Pecking Order" This Pecking Order Instinct is common even within the smallest of human herds, the immediate family. In general we might think of the Pecking Order Instinct as a rather benign instinct, but we would be wrong in this assumption, as wrong as wrong can be. Within human kind the Pecking Order Instinct exhibits itself throughout the whole gamut of human conflict ranging from the bickering between siblings to those most bizarre of human actions, including violent murder. It might be difficult to comprehend, but almost all of human conflict at every level and especially conflict between individuals has its base cause in the Pecking Order Instinct. It is an instinct whose tentacles stretch into some of the most morbid and bizarre aspects of human emotions.

Pecking orders are most clearly delineated within the individual members of the smallest herds. Within small groups, pecking orders that have been in place for long periods of time are usually very strongly established. They can be the cause of serious unrest and physical struggling, particularly if an outsider tries to become a member of the group. Only if the outsider is clearly seen by all of the members of the group as fitting into the lowest rank of their pecking order, and only if the outsider is willing to accept that lowest position, will they be easily accepted by the group. Their acceptance at the lowest level effectively moves everyone within the group, one notch up in the ranking of the pecking order ladder. Within the smallest of herds, the family, we can see the frequent battles among siblings to establish their supremacy over their brothers and/or sisters. This kind of sibling in-fighting necessarily continues for as long a time as it takes for the individuals to establish their ranking and their acceptance of their ranking within the group. Many times, too often in fact, some siblings are unable to accept any ranking within their group of siblings, which would make them to be of a lesser rank than that of another sibling. In such cases, the in-fighting continues throughout their childhood, and as we know is sometimes true, the in-fighting continues throughout most, if not all, of their adult life. Most of us have seen the continuous fighting that sometimes goes on between brothers or between sisters, the fighting is continuous simply because the individuals are unwilling to accept a lower pecking order ranking than that of their sibling, and so, the battling, being instinctively driven, goes on-and-on. It is common to see the inevitable conflict between parents and child, which begins when a teenager within a family comes into their time of sexual maturity. It is a conflict within the family, which is solely about a perceived challenge to the family's long established pecking order of its members. It is not too uncommon to see the Instinctive Pecking Order battle being continually waged between a husband and wife, when neither of them is willing to accept any kind of dominance by the other. Realize that almost all of those little verbal squabbles that we have with our peers are caused by our Pecking Order Instinct exercising its prerogative to test and see if we can take their place on the next rung up on the pecking order ladder. Among some of the less socially restrained creatures of nature, we often see that the struggle between siblings to establish their pecking order ranking, more often than not, results in the death of one or more of the physically weaker siblings. Sometimes death is also the result of humans struggling to establish their place within the pecking order. Pecking order struggles a usually taken too lightly, whenever there is not any sign of freely flowing blood, but those battles to establish a pecking order within a family or on a school playground can leave unhealthy burses on the psyche of those who are physically or mentally beaten down. The Pecking Order Instinct is extremely difficult to sidetrack, its battles will usually continue independent of the efforts to stop them, the best that can usually be done is to separate the combatants as a means of temporarily tempering their instinctive desires.

The Pecking Orders Instinct is an extremely primitive and natural way of establishing a quasi-peaceful order within a group by means of creating a recognized hierarchy of individuals, an order that excludes the chaos, which would surely result if anarchy reined.

The Instinct to Bully should not be confused with the Pecking Order Instinct, which is about establishing an individual's hierarchal ranking within a herd. The Instinct to Bully also should not be confused with the Put-Down Instinct, whose primary mechanism is speech and does not usually involve physical threats to an individual. The Instinct to Bully finds some resonance in each of us, but in most persons it is a weakly held instinct, which is usually sacrificed in the name of social harmony. But in some few persons, the Instinct to Bully is both a strong and a lasting emotion. Those persons who bully others gain some personal satisfaction from tormenting, intimidating, and threatening other persons. Bullies tend to gravitate into bullying just those persons, whom they discover are susceptible to being bullied, by means of first testing them with some initial intimidation. Once a bully has discovered those persons, who will allow themselves to be the bully's victim, the bully happily exerts upon them, at every opportunity, every kind of humiliation. In some bullies, the Instinct to Bully, is such a strong and dominant part of their basic character that they are doomed to be bullies for their entire lifetime, but there are also those bullies, where the instinct is not so strongly embedded into their character, and with a bit if forceful confronting, they are willing to keep the instinct subdued.

Every individual creature that is conscious of their living existence, instinctively and naturally believes that they are the center of their universe. It is clearly the result of a simple and powerful rational logic. All of a creature's senses clearly and unambiguously communicate to them that everything in existence is spread evenly across a landscape in which they alone are at its center. Clearly written in our kind's past history, this instinct has sometimes shown some of the quite laughable consequences, which oftentimes result when this instinct is coupled with a general righteous ignorance. The Self-Centered Instinct is what drove the Catholic Church to sternly maintain its ignorant fight against those enlightened thinkers who proposed that the Earth was not necessarily the center point about which all things celestial revolved. Still in today's world we see those persons and institutions who allow this instinct to go to their head, and then they deal with the world as if it was solely orbital to their own wants and needs. All children are instinctively prone to believe that their position in life is central, and all of their wants and needs should gravitate to them. It takes some time for children to learn that they are not in fact the center of all things, but are just a part of the all of life, and as an individual they must compete, like everyone else, for their time at center stage. Persons who strongly express the Self Centered Instinct are likely to become active in any areas of work where they can dominantly be the center of attention, so they gravitate to those professions which can best satisfy their desires, they become actors, singers, musicians, politicians and the like. Some persons who are strongly self centered are without the talents to fit into a profession that can give them the attention, which could satisfy them and so they are driven into satisfying there instinct by becoming an attention getting disruptive element in society.

COMMON ONLY TO OUR KIND

The Instinct of Mystic Attraction is very strange in that, in the general sense, it appears to have no specific benefit towards our survival. It would seem this instinct has no benefit for either the individual or the tribe or a modern society. It is within itself, almost mystical that it exists. But it does exist, and from an early age it reveals itself in our love of fairy tales, all kinds of magic, and in our belief in multitudes of nonmaterial things, which are beyond verification by using any logical means of testing them. The Instinct of Mystic Attraction is a powerfully strong instinct common to all societies throughout the world and has been present during all of known times, and it is because of this commonality within all societies that we have the right to see it as an instinctive condition. Like all instincts, it is present, more or less, to some degree even within those persons who are well educated and whom we might believe should be immune from believing in unverifiable fantasies. In every society, we see its presence is reveled by a multitude of stories and beliefs, which had their origin in ancient times, but there are many mythical beliefs whose origin is quite recent. The Instinct of Mystic Attraction ranges to include beliefs in: fairy tales, creatures of make-believe such as ghost and goblins, all kinds of magic and tales of magic, flying saucers, telepathy, teleportation, religions, miracles, fortunetellers and other kinds of prophesy, psychics, astrology, ritualistic behaviors, and many, many others. The only commonalties, between the various manifestations of this instinct are that their basic elements are not verifiable in the natural world, and they appear to be creations of our very creative imagination. Such an instinct would seem not to be survivable within a wild environment, where the evolutionary justice of surviving is all about selecting traits that directly contribute to survivability. What we might guess we have going here, which allows this Instinct of Mystical Attraction to exist and thrive is the result and a minor consequence of some other human characteristic, which is itself a powerful contributor to our survival. It is likely that the primary element that secondarily spawns this instinct is our creative thinking, which has been a most powerful instrument for our survival. Creative thinking leads naturally to all kinds of creations, creations that are applicable to the real world, and are applicable to the pleasures of the arts and to other creations that do not necessarily make any contributions to either. Creative thinking certainly is the provider of the elements, that are the ethereal substances, which this instinct embraces, but it does not give us a clue as to the instinct's origin. I think it would be a good bet that the mystic instinct survives only at the wellspring of its primary source, but its actual origins like the instinct itself remain illusive and mystifying.

We should be somewhat amazed, at the high position of common acceptance some of the elements of this Mystic Instinct have assumed within the present world.

Among all human societies there exists within each of them an instinct to make or see the events of nature and our history as cyclic. The naturally observable cyclic motions of the objects of our solar system have so powerfully influenced the development of many instincts within our and other species, that humans are prone to make or to see many events as cyclic, even when we must go to illogical extremes to do so. The movement of the moon as it regularly repeats its phases of light cycles, has embedded its harmonic cycles within our instinctive structures and these instincts, whose causative triggers are tied to the moon's cycles, have a profound influence upon the instinctive reproductive cycles of many animals. The cyclic daily appearance and disappearance of the sun has written its cyclic pattern into our instincts, which drive our daily rhythms, they influence the times when we are awake or asleep, when we hunt or work, and when we desire to eat. Some ancient societies had mystical cycles related to their calendars, which at certain regular times where supposed to predict the earth or its population was to be destroyed and then again reconstructed in a series of never ending cycles. We have invented unnatural cycles as a part of our calendars, centuries and millennia, which have no natural significance whatsoever, and yet there are always those among us who confess, they can see that some monumental event will happen at the beginning or ending of these unnatural human made imaginary cycles of time. The cycles of the objects of the nearby solar system have so indelibly been written into many of our instincts, that we are willing to see, find, or make events cyclic, which cannot by any logical interpretation be known as real and natural cyclic events.

There is a strong possibility that for humans, we instinctively treat our long held beliefs, as if they are a real physical appendage of our material bodies. Consider what the situation is, when anyone makes a challenge to one of your long held beliefs. If the belief is strongly held, you fight against any attempt to change it. No matter how numerous and logical are the arguments for changing a belief that has been held for a long time, many people will mount a serious and sometimes completely irrational fight against changing it. They will even mount a fight that is totally without any supporting logic. They may become so emotionally aroused that even the Savage Instinct might become activated. It is quite obvious that the resistance this instinct blindly asserts against change is equivalent to the kind of struggle that we might expect to be mounted, if someone were trying to remove by amputation their hand, or their arm, or leg. This Instinct is one that is the basic cause for some of the most serious problems of conflict within and between herds and among the individuals that are their members.

Without much doubt, for humans, there exist an instinct that leads us to believe that the future is pregnant with some kind of mythical hope of a better time to come. This instinct is very much involved with the "Instinct to Survive." The Optimistic Instinct is surely what has been the source of the magical encouragement for our kind to believe, that we can survive, even against death itself.

THE MAGNIFIED
INSTINCTS

It would be reasonable to wonder at a rather strange situation. In modern society, we all have witnessed that certain games of sport are able to command the attendance of remarkably large crowds that come to observe the game's playing. Many sports can sometimes draw a large audience, but there are some sports that consistently draw huge crowds. All of these sports are involved in the control of some projectile, usually a ball. If you were an alien visitor to our world, and you were a witness to these sporting events, I'm sure you would be puzzled as to how the apparently simple manipulation of a projectile could be of such great interest to all of those people who come to see it. I believe it can only be explained by remembering that the instinctive ability to throw and quite accurately control a projectile was an important primary factor, which strongly contributed to our survival during primitive times. You might think of it this way: If in the prehistoric past a member of your tribe was a superbly accurate thrower of various kinds of projectiles, your tribe probably had, every day, some kind of meat to eat, and as a consequence your whole tribe was one that was likely to be well nourished and therefore its members were likely to survive through difficult times. **There is certainly something primitive and instinctive inside of us that drives us to worship at the "Shrines of the Controlled Projectile."** We pay our highest and special worship to those within a sport's team who are appointed to execute the most accurate control of a particular sport's projectile. We can gain some further insight into the near religious reverence some societies of the past have paid to those teams whose accurate control of a projectile successfully won the game, and also see the overwhelming disdain shown to the members of the loosing team. In the various different indigenous civilizations that thrived in Mesoamerica, the team winners of their infamous ball game were given great honors, while the members of the loosing team were summarily and ceremoniously murdered.

The precise accurate control of hand thrown projectiles represents a miraculous refinement of the instincts, which control the basic movements of the muscles, which are the active primary driving force behind the throw. In the game of basketball the arching flight of a three-point basketball shot requires very special fine-tuning of the instinctive actions, which basically drive the shot. And that fine-tuning has been learned and acquired from many, many, hours of practicing these shots. The basketball shooter's brain certainly does not solve, in terms of mathematics, the differential equations that could lead to the muscle control for defining the acceleration and the angle of the ball's departure to sink the basket. But what the basketball shooter's brain instead does is, it has learned primarily from visual experience the images associated with the positions of the ball as it is accelerated downwards by the force of gravity and how the ball's forward flight duration interacts to define the ball's complete trajectory and by these means the shooter's brain visually models the muscle dynamics which finely-tune the muscle's controlling instincts to reproduce in reality the image that the brain has modeled. A startling consequence of this method of matching the brains constructed visual image of how the successful shot should be executed, is that the basketball shooter knows immediately after only a very few moments from the time the ball has left their hand, if, or if not their shot will be successful. And they are able to know this with certainty because they can immediately see if the balls flight exactly matches the correct trajectory of the image of its flight that was constructed within their brain before the shot was executed.

At a very early age, children delight in the discovery of their personal ability to throw things. We all delight in the exhibition of throwing being done with great accuracy; we especially enjoy seeing it done by teams representing our group, tribe, city, or nation. Some of the most useful weapons of the pre-modern and modern times are those machines, which hurl an object or are themselves hurled for a great distance. The Roman's siege machines, which could quite accurately hurl flaming pitch or huge stones over or through the protective walls of a fortress, were the ultimate terror weapon of their time. Today the gun is the ultimate personal projectile thrower and it pretty much brings everyone who possesses a gun into equality with any and every other kind of projectile thrower.

We should give a bit of thought about the possible evolutionary path that has lead us to be able to vocalize the audio patterns that are the symbols of our complex spoken language. Consider the high probability that in humans, as well as in all of the other creatures of nature, who to one degree or another make vocalizations, that their vocalizing is an instinctive part of their nature. Surely the ability to communicate by using vocalized audio patterns must have very slowly evolved along with the physical biological structures, which taken together form the biological systems that make audio communication possible. From the historical evidence, we see that spoken language always precedes all other language forms, except body language. There was not suddenly one day when we as humans generated a series of sequential sounds that were representative of a complex spoken language. Our ability to communicate with each other by means of a spoken language could only be realistically accomplished by our kind, in the first instance, by our instinctive drive to make simple sounds, the same kinds of simple sounds, which many of the other creatures of nature are able to generate by using their extremely rudimentary vocal structures. Every type of intelligible communication with your own kind, and also with other kinds of creatures, no matter how limited in scope, gives your kind a distinct advantage at surviving in nature. Communication, particularly vocal communication, which has the distinct advantage of being intelligible at quite a long distance and to places that might be out of view, is a very powerful kind of communicating, which is over and above the power of communicating by using only body language or other visual signals. True, visual signaling has an advantage of being silent, but in general, in primitive times, it was highly limited in the complexity of its possible communications. We are all aware that many of the creatures of nature have the ability and do communicate by means of sound, but most of those other creature's communications are solely of a very limited and basic nature. The ability to make different complex vocalized sounds, which have a specific meaning, is without much argument of a great value to a creature as a contributor to their survival. Since the ability to make complex vocalizations is predetermined by the physical system, which facilitates vocalization, it is certain that evolutionary processes were at work continually selecting for better physical systems, and selecting as a precondition of survival, those creatures that could make the best use of them. It's a reasonable assumption that the Instinct to Speak is one that naturally developed as nature selected for those creatures that were able to take advantage of using complex vocal communications, which contributed to their survival. It was a cyclic process that was self-reinforcing, a process of nature selecting for increasingly complex physical vocalizing systems, coupled with selecting those particular individuals who were the most capable of making intelligible vocalizations. **It is probably not an unreasonable speculation that speech was one of the most powerful elements in driving natural selection towards selecting for those individuals who could make use of it by devising ever more complex audio codes for communicating.**

Every known human society, independent of the period in which it exists or has existed, has, or had its own spoken language, and so there are thousands of uniquely different spoken languages. This seems to be good evidence that "To

Speak" is an instinctive trait. Speaking is common among all humans although what is spoken (the language) has the greatest variations of all human characteristics. Speaking or vocalizing is common among most complex creatures of nature, but none of the other creatures of nature can compare to the masterful complex vocalizations, which humans perform as a means of communicating by using their indigenous language. The fact that many other creatures of nature "Speak" and by this means are able to make some limited communications with their own kind, seems in itself to be good evidence that "Speaking" is truly of an instinctive nature as it is spread across much of the animal kingdom. While to speak is certainly instinctive, language certainly is not instinctive. Even when the ability to vocalize is at its most rudimentary stage, and a creature is only able to utter the most basic and primitive of sounds, the ability to relate those sounds, in a symbolic way, to some thing or an event is a learned ability. Language, even its most basic form, for every creature, is acquired through learning, not by instinct.

Within human populations the intensity for expressing the Instinct to Speak varies over a broad range, at one end of the spectrum of the intensity to speak are those persons who always need to be prodded to say even a very few words and who are quite willing to remain speechless unless they are forcibly coaxed into speaking. At the other end of the spectrum, which represents the intensity of the Instinct to Speak, are those persons who are essentially unable to ever stop talking as long as there is any audience within a listening distance. The intensity for expressing the Instinct to Speak for most persons lies somewhere between these two extremes of intensities.

Curiosity is an instinct, which is broadly dispersed throughout many of the creatures of the animal kingdom. It is an instinct whose near magical power, when unrestrained can lead a creature to either life benefiting discoveries or to a sudden death; therefore nature has necessarily modulated the Curiosity Instinct with restraint. The strength of the expression of the Curiosity Instinct in humans is many orders of magnitude stronger than it is within any other of nature's creatures. For most of nature's creatures the Curiosity Instinct is only intense enough to be able to satisfy their need for food, water, shelter, or sex. Just how strong or restrained an individual is at expressing this instinct is, like other instincts, fixed before the time of their birth. At one end of this instinct's intensity spectrum are those persons whose curiosity is both weak and short lasting, and at the other end of the spectrum are those persons whose curiosity will not easily be satisfied until they have discovered every ramification about the situation or about some object of their curiosity. Instinctive curiosity within some few members of the human population is so strong, so dogging, and has so much depth, they will tenaciously and continually follow a trail, whose every part lies deeply hidden below the visible surface of nature's magical real world. As it is the usual situation for any instinct, the intensity for the expression of the Curiosity Instinct by any individual within the general population, lies somewhere between these two extremes.

To very young children most every part of the real world is opaque to their senses, but curiosity about those few things they can discern, inevitably leads to further discovery, learning, and remembering what they have discovered. And those memories of things discovered begin to give curiosity a generalized direction, which can begin to lay down the beginning foundations, which might point out the direction of a child's future interests. And these interests can draw a child's curiosity into an ever-narrowing field of specific interest, where more and more discoveries are made. And so by means of curiosity and discovery complementing and reinforcing each other, we are most of us gently directed to what we claim are our particular interests in life. For some persons their interests are tightly focused but for most persons their interest lie within the common general interests of their peers and with little or no extreme interest in any few particular aspects of life. But for all of us, the feedback of those things we discovered during our first childhood curiosities directly begins our journey of discovery throughout our life. It is because of how our instinctive curiosity begins to direct our learning and interests, that children must have a learning environment, which is vastly richer in opportunities for attracting their curiosity than any of the severely limited environments which society's educational systems currently are willing to provide for our children.

It is a part of the basic nature of curiosity as it resides in any creature and especially within humans, that everything of any and every kind that is unnaturally hidden or forbidden, are the particular things we are forever infatuated with discovering, and there are always those persons, who are willing to risk and pay any cost for attaining the discovery. Therefore for any ignorant group that has the power to forbid to us what they do not desire us to know, is an act of forbidding, which is within itself a self-defeating act. Because to forbid some discovery, causes it to become like a self directing beacon, whose ever present light draws us, like moths, to its forbidden light and we become addicted to discovering its forbidden nature and are nearly helpless to ignore the forbidden beckoning.

For humans and some other creatures there are some strange twists to the simple Curiosity Instinct, one such twist is a morbid curiosity that draws us like a magnetic force to all kinds of things and events that are morbid in nature. The more morbid the situation, the more strongly we are drawn to dote over it. This instinctive drawing to morbid scenes can be seen in such simple events as the extreme slowing of traffic as it approaches the site of a vehicle accident. The traffic always slows so people can gawk at the accident even though the accident is in no way physically blocking the roadway. Stories that are extremely morbid in their nature are always the top sellers for newspapers and other news media. There are newspapers whose main theme for generating profit is their dedication to exploiting the public's morbid curiosity. Stories that are considered to be a high watermark of morbidity, such as, the "Jack the Ripper" story, are repeated over and over throughout near history. The story of "Dr. Frankenstein" has been an extraordinary morbid delight ever since its creation. Any examination of the stories that have been the greatest monetary successes of our times will reveal that a great number of them are steeped in a morbid tale. Consider Frankenstein, Dracula, The Mummy, Aliens, and even the recent motion picture story of the sinking of the Titanic, which many persons would consider to be a pure love story, but if the same love story were told without the morbid backdrop of the multitude of lives that were lost in the dramatic sinking, then the story would have only been mediocre at best. Young persons swarm to movies that are bathed in bloodshed and horrible deaths.

We are hopefully curious about what primitive mechanism might be beneath this morbid curiosity. It must have, in some way, been a strong factor, which contributed to our survival. Most likely, in the distant past it was this morbid curiosity that drew our kind to the scenes of the dying and death, where we could as scavengers possibly find food. We couldn't smell the distant scent of blood or battle in the air like many other scavengers can smell these odors. But whenever, we heard the chaotic sounds of a distant struggle, we must have surely been drawn nearby to await the outcome and the food scrapes it might provide. Since we are, most of us, quite well fed, we no longer attempt to feast at the morbid sites that have drawn our attention.

Many animals that are carnivores also harbor a strong morbid curiosity, and this simple attraction to a nearby site of a chaotic struggle and death, has allowed them the opportunity to obtain the food leftovers as a contribution towards their survival.

We should not be too upset by the fact that we are drawn to morbid scenes. The magnet that draws us there is surely within our genes, it is something that we cannot escape. It does not mean that by this morbid attraction, this instinctive curiosity, we are susceptible to committing morbid atrocities. It is the "Savage Instinct" that we must be concerned about in that respect. Morbid curiosity is itself a benign trait.

Humans are nearly alone in the animal kingdom in demonstrating their Instinct to Organize. Although the Instinct to Organize shows itself in human populations as exemplifying the full spectrum of it's possible intensities, it is present in all off us at least to some degree. We can see in every human society that this instinct relentlessly drives people to attempt to logically organize, in some ranking or another, everything they observe, including physical objects and ideas. **This Instinct to Organize should rank near to the top of the list of those human attributes, which have most strongly contributed to our great successes in discovering, learning, surviving, and thriving within the world.** By logically organizing related patterns which have been discovered in the world, any unusual or missing pattern cries out its condition from amongst the other members of its grouping, and it is thereby brought to a powerful scrutiny, as a means of discovering why it is different or missing from the grouping. Within the power of observing any organized grouping, is the ability to infer the most reasonable nature of the object, pattern, which is missing from the grouping. By means of observing the pattern that is before the missing pattern and the pattern that comes after the missing pattern, it is logical to assume that the missing pattern is of a median form to those it lies between. Humans attempt to organize all things, including their ideas and philosophies. They will organize objects by color, size, shape, weight, taste, or by whatever special properties they can conjure up. Human's compulsive organizing ranges from arranging their scientific ideas into tables and graphs to the simple organizing of the clothes in their closets and all things between these to extremes. Humans organize, organize, and organize, and to do it is our natural instinctive compulsion.

CONCLUSIONS

We have here touched upon just few of the instincts that guide us in our daily endeavors. We should realize that many of our instincts are shared in common with other creatures including some creatures that are our most distant relatives. Those instincts, which are apart of us are always present to some degree in all humans, and are sometimes common among all members of a different species. How many different species have an instinct that they share in common, gives us an indication of how far back in time the instinct originated.

Instincts basically are all simple or complex reflex loops, whose triggering cause and effect relationships are deterministic, but the secret power of some creatures is that the creature's memories can change the nature of some of the instinct's cause and effect relationships, enhancing the instinct, diminishing the instinct, or completely subduing the instinct for some determined amount of time. We should realize that those memories, which can directly modulate the different instinctive mechanisms, were all formed by the creature's intelligence systems, whose senses scan the environment and cause any logical event they find there to be registered in the creature's memory, so in the best sense the logic of the natural environment copies itself into a creature's memory and those memories which are appropriate can then influence the functioning of the creature's various instinctive mechanisms.

An individual's instincts begin to be fine-tuned by means of learning from the time of their birth and continuing throughout their lifetime. Those persons who are present during your early life, parents, relatives, friends, and especially teachers strongly influence the refining control of your instinctive nature.

Most of our inherited instincts lie within us as hidden good spirits that secretly direct every physical action and nearly every mental aspect of our lives. Some of our instincts pose more danger to a peace loving society and our world than they are of any value to our civilized world of today, and those instincts which are obviously detrimental to our personal life and our society's well being need to be modified by learning to be self attenuated or to be completely subdued.

From the time of our birth there are conditions, which we instinctively perceive as desirable or undesirable. These predetermined instinctive likes and dislikes have always been important for our immediate survival, and they are easily understood as either presenting some threat, or some promised nurturing to our well-being. They are some of our most basic sensory survival instincts, which react to: sweet and sour, warmth or cold, comfort or pain, hunger or satiety, light or darkness, suffocation or free breathing, pungent odor or sweet odor, and a slowly evolving gentle sound or a suddenly loud sound. We sometimes think of these most basic instinctive reactions in terms of the situations that produced the reaction, as being "Good" or "Bad." It seems possible that these instincts are the beginning elements of our many extended ideas about all of those more removed situations, which we associate with being either good, or bad.

There should be some suspicion at least for humans, that there are many instinctive biases within us from the time of our birth. These are biases that affect our lifetime interests, and in some strange and fateful way they guide us along a path that we joyfully follow. Sometimes, it seems, some people from the time of their birth, were meant to be an artist, a naturalist, a teacher, a dancer, an athlete, a joyous person, or a joyless person. Sometimes we see a person has become mis-directed, and then we can see those persons who maybe should have been a doc-tor but work at soldiering, a potential scientist who works at manual labor, the would be actor who is a fireman, and in this world of maladaptation, we have people unhappily wandering through life trying to survive in a profession where they find no real joy or happiness and some people are without any instinctive biases, which can direct their personal desires, and much of the cause of this problem can be laid upon the serious lack of possible options for stimulating their interest during the time they were growing through childhood towards adult-hood. It is obvious that children of the same parents can be markedly different in their personalities, the strength of their instincts, and to what they are naturally attracted. Some of the cause of this is simply because of the happenstances within their young environment. Of course some of the cause of sibling differences is simply because of the naturally occurring variations, which come about during the exceeding complex duplication of the individual's basic genetic material. None of us, not even so-called identical twins, are actually genetically identical and so we should not be at all surprised that the children from common parents are usually noticeably different from one another in their interests and likes and dislikes.

Sometimes things that at first observation appear to be the most obvious, sim-ple, and without underlying depth, are things that can subtly connect to a much larger meaning. I suspect this is true for all of the hidden instincts that are certainly associated with the simplest patterns displayed by the many life forms of nature that we detect with our senses.

It is of considerable importance, we make a major effort to discover those parts of our human actions, which are truly instinctive and separate from those that are learned. There may well be many instincts that lie hidden within us and only require some catalytic agent, physical, chemical, or cultural, to trigger their emergence. And it would also seem quite certain that many of the unusual and extreme mental deviations expressed by some individuals within the population, which are so different from those discernable within the majority of the population, are possibly in existence simply because those few individuals have very sensitive levels for the triggering of certain instincts, these are instincts, which for most individuals within the population require relatively high levels of sensory stimulations to trigger them.

We should think about the array of inherited mechanisms, which generate those very special regulating chemical protein substances that flow within our blood streams. Their chemicals are of equal importance to our normal functioning as are our inherited instincts. In a sense those mechanisms, which synthesize the controller chemicals circulating in our blood stream directly affect the quality, strength, and functioning of our inherited instincts, and the quality and quantity of our other mental activities. These bodily-synthesized chemicals are in some respects the primal conditioning agents for all of the body's functions. These inherited mechanisms of chemical synthesis and their products affect every aspect of our outlook on life by applying their own special kind of fine-tuning to our instincts, which directly affect how we perceive the real and the imaginary world. These chemical mechanisms affect our level and balance between curiosity and fear, love and hatred, happiness or sadness. They can make the sunny or cloudy day of our inner-environment.

With some small consideration, we can understand why some economic systems are the most stable, long lasting, and successful. The reasons for their success are because they include within the tenets of their structures those elements that both respect and feed upon our natural instinctive biases.

We also need to realize within the complexities of instincts, instincts can combine their observable expression to yield a new expression, which might appear as uniquely different from either of the two parent instincts. Some of the instincts, which have herein been portrayed as the expression of individual instincts might in fact be compounded from other independent instincts.

It is a reasonable assumption, that there are at least as many instincts, which have been as powerful a contributor to our success in Mother Nature's world, as are any other aspects of our nature, physical, or mental. We have said much about instincts being inheritable, and we have lain heavily upon the idea that the strength of expression of an instinct, for any individual, lies somewhere within a spectrum where is represented all of its possible intensities of expression. These spectrums, representing all of the possible strengths of expression of an instinct, can graphically be represented as lying within a bell curve. It is sure that the expression of any naturally inheritable feature can be organized to lie within the boundaries of some symmetrical bell curve. The "Universal Bell Curve" comes to us naturally as a mapping of the probability of the occurrences of certain natural random happenings, including those of heredity; there are some important conclusions to be made from this condition. Nature's wonderful inheritable physical and mental mechanisms, including the mechanisms of intelligence, consciousness, and instincts are common among all members of our species, and their power of expression within any individual lies somewhere within the spectrum, which represents all of their possible intensities of expression

Visualize for a moment that across the entire history of evolution, in the most general sense, for any given time, the strength of expression and the commonality of instincts from creature to creature can be visualized as a slowly and smoothly changing function. Even in our present world for every creature, except for humans, these relationships between different creature's instincts and the power of their expression is clearly a slowly changing relationship. But in humans, we can see a nearly explosive difference in the power of the expression of some of our instincts as compared to all other animals. As just a few examples, in humans the Curiosity Instinct is a thousand times more powerfully expressed than it is in any other kind of creature. The Instinct to Organize is a thousand times more powerful in humans and we are hard pressed to show its existence to any mentionable degree in any other creature. The instinct to Nurture, although strong in some other creatures, is a thousand times more powerful in humans than in our nearest animal competitor. The Instinct to Build is a thousand times more powerfully expressed in our kind as exemplified by the unbelievable great variety and complexity of the constructions, which we are ever building. The Instinct of Ownership is a thousand times more powerful for humans. The Instinct to Compete is a thousand times more powerfully expressed within humans, where in the other creatures of nature, competition is generally limited to struggling for the favors of a sexual mate or struggling at obtaining food. The Instinct to Speak is a thousand times more powerful in humans.

Between us and the other animals, how could these great discontinuities of the magnitude of an instinct's expression have arisen within our kind?

These most unusual differences in the power of an instinct's expression would seem to only be explainable by some major cataclysmic event within Mother Nature's environment. This is certainly not what happen. We should be willing to speculate that **sometimes very minor mutations can be the triggering agent which powerfully points the way down a new evolutionary pathway, where selection of the fittest to survive is not primarily determined by a creature's physical aspects, but instead by the more intangible nature of how the creature's unusually enhanced instincts are themselves the mechanisms, which by the results of their survival successes drive towards the natural selection of evermore enhanced instincts.** What might have been the primary trigger that led our kind down an avalanching path of more and more powerfully expressing some of our inherited instincts? **That triggering event most likely was a mutation that enhanced our Curiosity Instinct, and from just this cause, it is believable than the eventual conclusion is what we see within our present characteristic nature.**

I also propose, **this group of instincts whose expression has been so powerfully enhanced, are the more primary determiners of our successes within the natural environment, than are any of our physical features, including those features that gave us the potential for bipedal walking, or the marvelous dexterity of the human hand, or any other physical features of our kind. Our Ape cousins have good approximations of these same physical features, but there is not the same comparison, between their achievements in the natural world and our achievements.** This should alert any thinking person in to looking more seriously at the magnificent power of our inherited instincts.

Here is one last idea to which we should give some considerate thought. **We should be seriously tempted into seeing all of the structures and functions of the human brain as being naturally mutated neural structures which straddle the primitive junction points which are the natural inflection points where an instinct's sensory neural inputs junction to become an instinct's active neural outputs.** In my coming book "Consciousness and Intelligence" this concept about the true nature of the brain will be explored in detail.

As concerns humankind's nature, there are institutions that would lead us to believe about ourselves what is not in fact true about our instinctive nature. They would like to convince us that we are creatures of some divine plan of creation and that we are somehow a part of all they see as morally good, while at the same time leading us into denying our true nature, that we are creatures of the animal world, originally wild fierce creatures, who have been selected by Mother Nature's laws of survival to be all that we really are.

The simple and truthful realization of what we are, and how we got to where we are within nature's world, is the ultimate truth that any philosophy could ever propose to know. It is ultimately the most powerful state that any human mind can ever attain. It is a true kind of nirvana. It is with this knowing state of mind that we can make ever new beginnings and provide for a future where our chances are best for surviving whatever random hells, which nature will with great certainty rise up against us. The fact that we might have to eventually face up to what we are as completely definable creatures in terms of a very complex arranged organization of billions of very simple structures is not in anyway whatsoever a degradation of the truth of our humanity. Understanding what we are has led us to realizing both the miraculous and morally good achievements of our kind and to understanding the nature of our more hidden ugly and evil natures. Understanding frees us from worshiping at false shrines in hopes of saving some part of us that does not now exist, but allows us to ever strive within the reaches of reality to work at obtaining all we can dream for a better world.

For our kind we can hopefully realize in the truest sense, throughout the brief history of life, all of the creatures of life are the wind beneath our wings, because we share so much in common with them. We must ultimately make our understandings to be a triumph for all creatures. And pray, that humankind is increasingly successful in its hopeful search for survival against the Forces of Chaos and the Hidden Spirits that Drive Us.

◆   ◆   ◆

We should realize that very much of what we are, as creatures within nature, is defined within the boundaries of intelligence, instincts, and those things that we have learned from experience and by being educated.

0-595-28278-4

www.ingramcontent.com/pod-product-compliance
Lightning Source LLC
Chambersburg PA
CBHW020302290526
45784CB00003B/1328